# The
# Digital Prince
Leadership Strategies
for the Modern World

By
Patrick H. Eldridge

# The
## Digital Prince
Leadership Strategies
for the Modern World

# Table of Contents

# Introduction

In an era where smartphones are our trusted companions and social media platforms are the town squares, the intricacies of leadership have taken on new dimensions. The world has shifted dramatically since Niccolò Machiavelli penned his insights on power and politics, yet the essence of his teachings continues to reverberate across centuries. Today's leaders find themselves navigating a mosaic of digital landscapes where influence is measured in likes and retweets, and power is no longer restrained by geographical borders. This book seeks to illuminate the path for modern leaders, extracting and reimagining Machiavellian principles to suit the pulsating rhythms of the digital age.

The digital transformation is not just a change in tools or technologies—it's a fundamental shift in how we experience human connection, access information, and understand our world. In this context, leadership demands a recalibration, an alignment with the velocity and volatility of digital currents. We stand at the confluence of technology and humanity, where the traditional tenets of leadership evolve to meet the demands of a hyperconnected society. This introduction aims to lay out the landscape, articulating why such a recalibration is essential and how this book endeavors to equip leaders with the necessary skills to thrive in this environment.

Power, in its essence, remains timeless. It motivates people, influences decisions, and propels movements forward. However, the channels through which power is wielded and perceived have transformed. Emerging technologies provide unprecedented opportunities for leaders to expand their influence beyond conventional boundaries. Yet, with these opportunities come complexities and challenges. Navigating these challenges requires more than mere adaptation; it calls for a profound understanding of the digital cosmos, where algorithms dictate visibility and data begets decisions. Herein lies the necessity for a new kind of Machiavellian insight, one grounded in the realities of our digital world.

In this digital renaissance, leaders must be as versatile as they are visionary, resilient as they are resourceful. Adaptation, once a luxury, is now a prerequisite for survival and success. The book you're about to delve into intricately bridges Machiavelli's incisive perspectives with the practicalities of contemporary digital leadership. It emphasizes not only the necessity of understanding power dynamics but also the strategic application of this understanding to fulfill organizational and personal objectives in the modern context.

Key to navigating the complexities of digital power is the ability to identify and map the networks and influencers that hold sway. The power structures of the past—based on location, wealth, or legacy—have been augmented by digital influences such as follower counts and engagement rates. Understanding these dynamics, and using them to one's advantage, requires a nuanced approach that balances traditional Machiavellian cunning with modern data analytics and strategic foresight.

Moreover, building influence today goes beyond crafting speeches or media appearances. It involves carefully curating a digital persona that resonates across various platforms—each with its norms and cultures. Social media, once seen as a supplementary tool, now stands at the forefront of influence. Leaders must master the art of modern persuasion, where authenticity and transparency are as crucial as rhetoric and narrative. Today's leaders must wield digital influence with a deft touch, mindful of both the opportunities and pitfalls at every digital intersection.

Effective communication in this digital era is another cornerstone of leadership. It is not solely about conveying information but about creating connections and fostering trust in a virtual realm often marred by anonymity and skepticism. The digital stage requires leaders to be genuine communicators, engaging with audiences substantively whilst being attuned to the instantaneous feedback cycle that digital platforms entail. This instantaneousness shapes the very fabric of decision-making processes, challenging leaders to sift through vast torrents of data to make informed, yet timely, decisions.

With the rapid accumulation of information comes the threat of overload, making the art of decision-making more crucial than ever. Balancing speed and accuracy in decisions dictates a leader's ability to remain robust in the face of adversity. Ethical considerations, too, take center stage— modern leaders must grapple with privacy concerns and find harmonious pathways that align profit with ethical responsibility. The digital age demands leaders to be astute decision-makers and ethical stewards, committed to transparency and sustainability.

As we journey further into the twenty-first century, the qualities that define exceptional leaders have evolved. Empathy, emotional intelligence, adaptability, and an unwavering commitment to learning have emerged as non-negotiable facets of effective leadership. Remote working environments, digital teams, and global connectivity necessitate leaders who can inspire and guide diverse teams—themes that this book will explore in depth. By understanding these dynamics and integrating digital tools and strategies, leaders can streamline operations and cultivate a culture of constant innovation.

Ultimately, this book envisions a future for leadership that embraces complexity rather than shies away from it, fostering a spirit of lifelong learning and innovation. It recognizes that while digital tools augment our abilities, the core essence of leadership—connection, vision, and influence—remains unchanged. By melding Machiavellian philosophies with modern digital strategies, it offers a roadmap for leaders seeking to make impactful and enduring changes in their spheres of influence.

The narratives of power and leadership are being rewritten, and at this pivotal juncture, embracing the interconnectedness of our world can create pathways to groundbreaking advancements and paradigms. As the digital age continues to unfold, the adaptations and insights offered in this book will equip you not just to navigate this new world, but to lead it with vision and courage. Prepare to embark on a journey of transformation—a journey that harnesses the past to effectively navigate the future.

# Chapter 1:
# Foundations of Digital Leadership

In an era where the digital landscape is molding the fabrics of society, leaders find themselves at a fascinating crossroads— a point requiring a fusion of ancient wisdom and modern ingenuity. This chapter delves into the essential foundations of digital leadership, urging readers to re-envision their strategies to adapt to the relentless, tech-driven world of today. It draws on Machiavellian principles, reexamining how his insights into power and strategy can be effectively harnessed in a time where influence wanders in fleeting moments across cyberspace. The successful digital leader combines the steadfast qualities of traditional leadership with nimble adaptability to digital trends, freeing themselves from the rigidity of hierarchy while embracing the fluidity of networks. In this dynamic realm, adaptability, foresight, and a keen understanding of digital cultures are pivotal. This foundational chapter lays the groundwork for mastering influence and power in the digital age, providing future-proof insights and direction for those determined to thrive in our hyperconnected world.

## The Digital Renaissance

The Digital Renaissance is more than just a metaphor; it's a seismic shift in how we perceive and engage with the world.

Just as the European Renaissance marked a period of profound cultural and intellectual transformation, today's digital shift unveils a vast realm of opportunities and challenges for modern leaders. It's an era characterized by the convergence of technology, creativity, and leadership, demanding new paradigms of thought and action.

In this burgeoning epoch, leaders are expected to evolve beyond traditional modes of operation. The static and hierarchical structures of the past are giving way to dynamic and interconnected networks. Leaders today must navigate with agility, leveraging digital tools to foster collaboration and drive innovation. The old adage "knowledge is power" takes on a new dimension in a world where information flows freely and ubiquitously.

Adapting to this new age is not optional but essential. The transformation requires a mindset that's both analytical and imaginative, capable of interpreting data while envisioning novel solutions. This digital shift calls for leaders to be both technologists and humanists, fully embracing the confluence of data and empathy to engender meaningful progress.

The principles of Machiavelli, which have echoed through centuries of leadership philosophy, find fresh relevance here. The strategic cunning, adaptability, and pragmatism he advocated are now essential in the face of digital disruption. "The ends justify the means," often attributed to Machiavelli's ruthless pragmatism, is reimagined in this context as leveraging digital means to achieve well-intentioned ends.

Yet, it's not just about harnessing technology; it's about cultivating a digital ethos. This ethos integrates ethics, innovation, and leadership to navigate the intricate web of digital existence responsibly. Leaders must balance the rapid pace of technological advancement with the enduring principles of integrity and human dignity. Ethical considerations in data usage, privacy, and digital rights are critical areas where leadership must not only respond but proactively shape policy and practice.

Consider the role of influence in the digital landscape. Traditional channels of power must adapt to a democratized environment where influence is both fluid and fleeting. Social media, digital platforms, and real-time communication have redistributed power, making it more accessible yet more transitory. Effective digital leaders understand the importance of building authentic and lasting connections through these platforms, resonating with audiences not just through authority but through genuine engagement.

The digital era also demands a renaissance in creative thinking. Innovation thrives at the intersections of diverse disciplines, and leaders must foster environments where such interdisciplinary collaboration is the norm. The blending of artificial intelligence, biotechnology, and digital art, among others, can lead to breakthroughs that redefine industries. Here, leadership is about inspiring teams to think beyond conventional boundaries and embrace a culture of continuous discovery and adaptation.

Moreover, the digital renaissance is reshaping how decisions are made. The sheer volume of data available to leaders is both a boon and a burden. Decision-making strategies must evolve to filter and interpret this data effectively, turning potential information overload into insightful action. Leaders must develop the acumen to not just follow data-driven insights but to question and contextualize them within broader human experiences.

It's also an era of increased vulnerability, where digital security becomes paramount. Leaders today must develop a robust understanding of cybersecurity, not only to protect organizational assets but to foster trust among stakeholders. The interconnected nature of digital networks means that breaches in one area can have ripple effects, emphasizing the need for comprehensive, proactive security strategies.

As leaders embrace the opportunities of the digital renaissance, they must also prepare for its challenges. Change is a constant in this context, demanding resilience and adaptability that go beyond mere survival toward thriving in uncertainty. This era is as much about building infrastructure as it is about building capacity—the capacity to innovate, to empathize, to lead in a world that's ceaselessly evolving.

In conclusion, the Digital Renaissance offers a landscape ripe with potential for those willing to reimagine leadership through a digital lens. It's an invitation to explore uncharted territories, to redefine power and influence in a world unbound by conventional limitations. Leaders poised to navigate this landscape will not only interpret change but will actively shape it, crafting legacies that align Machiavelli's timeless insights with the boundless possibilities of the digital age.

## Adapting Machiavelli to Modern Times

In today's world, where screens and technology frame the contours of our lives, Machiavelli's ancient wisdom seems both surprisingly relevant and in need of a reinterpretation. His writings, particularly "The Prince," offer timeless guidance on leadership and power, yet to apply these insights effectively, a nuanced understanding of contemporary dynamics is essential.

The realm of digital leadership is akin to Machiavelli's political landscapes—a place where stratagems, influence, and power are currency. Modern leaders, tasked with navigating this space, must become digital philosophers, wielding sticks and carrots not just in boardrooms but in the vast expanse of virtual domains. Here, strategy is everything, predicated on the delicate balance between asserting authority and maintaining ethical integrity.

Machiavelli argued that it is better to be feared than loved if you cannot be both. In the digital era, leaders must consider this old dichotomy with a fresh lens. Social media amplifies voices and opinions, making it crucial for leaders to inspire respect and trust rather than fear. Adapting this principle means cultivating a credible presence that fosters allegiance through engagement and authenticity.

Consider the art of crafting an online persona. It is not unlike the identity-building theories Machiavelli championed. Leaders must be seen as both relatable and formidable. Crafting a digital identity requires them to express personal values in ways that resonate with target audiences, embracing both transparency and strategic communication to build lasting influence.

Influence in the digital age is uniquely synergistic. Machiavelli's pragmatic views on human nature and alliances inform a current reality where digital influencers hold power akin to that of historical nobility. The modern Machiavellian leader is adept at networking, recognizing that fostering genuine connections is more impactful than transactional encounters.

Understanding power dynamics through a digital lens involves recognizing patterns and flows of information. Just as Machiavelli emphasized the importance of knowing oneself and one's adversaries, modern leaders must navigate big data adeptly, using information to anticipate trends and guide their decision-making processes strategically.

Moreover, the digital terrain demands ethical considerations—an area where Machiavellian adaptability is key. Navigating ethical challenges mirrors Machiavelli's reflections on virtù and fortuna, where virtual neighborhood exigencies call for quick, decisive adaptations that do not sacrifice core values.

Consider the balancing act of transparency and privacy. Machiavelli might argue that leaders need to control the narrative, ensuring that their actions are perceived positively. Today, with privacy concerns at the forefront, leaders must be masters of ethical transparency, ensuring they do not exceed the boundaries of public trust while leveraging transparency to maintain credibility.

Machiavelli's insights on adaptability in leadership predate our current climate's demands for constant learning and evolution. Digital leaders remain on the forefront of innovation, embracing change as a constant rather than a challenge. They nurture a culture of adaptability within their teams, ensuring everyone is prepared to pivot when new opportunities or obstacles arise.

The rapid pace of technological advancement is akin to the Renaissance spirit Machiavelli experienced, a rebirth of thought and exploration. Just as Machiavelli analyzed the intricacies of his time to develop strategies for rulership, modern leaders must remain students of technology, harnessing its potential without becoming enslaved by its whims.

With AI becoming more integrated into daily operations, the modern Machiavellian must rewrite the script to include empathy and human oversight in a world increasingly driven by data and algorithms. The question shifts from whether AI can replicate human abilities to how leaders can integrate these tools to enhance rather than replace human intuition and insight.

Ultimately, the key to adapting Machiavelli's insights to the digital era lies in synthesizing strategic acumen with ethical leadership. This synthesis entails understanding human motivations and digital mechanisms alike, translating ambitions into actions, and recognizing the importance of leading not from a place of control and manipulation but from influence and inspiration.

The journey of digital leadership continues with Machiavelli's echoes reverberating through strategy and reflection, offering lessons on power tempered with integrity and adaptability. This isn't about mirroring every principle from the past but evolving them to fit the distinct demands of our interconnected, digital tapestry.

As we navigate these modern times, Machiavelli helps us look beyond technology as merely a tool. Instead, it's a landscape—complex, multifaceted, and full of potential for those prepared to lead with vision, strategy, and a keen understanding of human dynamics augmented by digital advances. And in this landscape, the modern leader must not just survive but thrive, crafting a legacy that transcends screens and spans generations.

# Chapter 2:
# Understanding Digital
# Power Dynamics

In our modern digital arena, power dynamics appear not as linear hierarchies but as sprawling, intricate networks where influence isn't always about who holds the title but often about who captures the conversation. Navigating this complex web requires astute leaders to identify key influencers who shape narratives and map the digital networks that drive change. These influencers aren't just your loudest voices; they're the nodes in the network that, when examined closely, reveal the pathways of authority and persuasion. Digital power thrives on connectivity, adaptability, and the ability to sense subtle shifts in these networks, and as such, demands a nuanced understanding of both technology and human interaction. With a finger on the pulse of digital trends and an eye for potential tectonic shifts, today's leaders can master the art of digital influence, wielding it not just as a tool for growth but as a force for impactful, empathetic leadership. Recognizing where the power lies and how it flows in this digital landscape can be the key to unlocking unprecedented opportunities, ensuring you stand resilient amid the ever-shifting sands of the digital age.

## Identifying Key Influencers

In the realm of digital power dynamics, the art of identifying key influencers is akin to finding the linchpins in a complex network of connections. These individuals hold the invisible threads that weave through the vast digital tapestry, capable of amplifying messages, shaping opinions, and driving trends. Understanding who these digital influencers are, and how they operate, is crucial for any leader aspiring to wield power effectively in today's interconnected world.

Influencers come in myriad forms—ranging from social media personalities commanding millions of followers to niche bloggers whose opinions sway a specific community. They exert their influence not through hierarchical power, but through the trust and credibility they've built within their networks. The key is recognizing that these influencers can be hidden in plain sight, intertwined within digital networks in such a way that their impact is both subtle and profound.

The first step in identifying key influencers is acknowledging the various types of influence that exist. While some influencers work primarily by broadcasting to large audiences (often referred to as macro-influencers), others excel in niche areas, offering targeted impact that might not be immediately evident. These micro-influencers may not boast the largest follower counts, but their engagement levels and the authenticity they foster with their audience make their endorsements powerful.

Understanding the platforms where these influencers thrive is equally important. Different influencers can dominate distinct digital landscapes—some reigning over Twitter threads, others commanding attention on YouTube,

Instagram, or emerging platforms such as TikTok. Being platform-specific allows them to master the nuances of their chosen medium, creating content that resonates deeply with their audience. Leaders looking to engage with these influencers should first ensure they understand the unique characteristics and cultures of these platforms.

Beyond mere follower counts and engagement metrics, the true measure of an influencer's power lies in their ability to affect change. The influencers who can spark movements, incite dialogue, or shift public perception are those who possess a high degree of social capital. Social capital involves trust and the capacity to mobilize resources—whether human, intellectual, or financial—toward a given goal. It's this interplay between influence and social capital that modern leaders must scrutinize and appreciate.

However, identifying key influencers also involves understanding the digital ecosystems in which they reside. Networks, whether professional on LinkedIn or social on platforms like Instagram, are seldom linear. They can be diffuse, overlapping, and ever-shifting. Tools and analytics can aid in mapping these networks, offering insights into how information flows and pinpointing where influence is exerted most effectively. Utilizing these digital tools, leaders can discern patterns and predict who will emerge as the pivotal voices in discussions or trends.

Moreover, tapping into these influencers requires a keen sense of timing and adaptability. Digital landscapes are fast-paced environments where yesterday's trends can quickly become obsolete. Leaders need to not only identify but also build relationships with these influencers. This means engaging them in meaningful ways—whether through collaboration, dialogue, or co-creation of content—that recognize and honor their contribution to the broader digital discourse.

An understanding of digital body language is an emerging yet critical component here. The nuances of communication—enthusiasm expressed through emojis, likes, and retweets—can offer insights into the influencer's intentions and sentiments. Grasping these subtleties allows leaders to align themselves more strategically with influencers whose values and visions reflect their own. It's about connecting on a deeper level beyond transactional engagements.

No less important is the ethical aspect of working with influencers. The integrity and transparency with which these relationships are managed can significantly affect public perception. Leaders should be aware of potential pitfalls—such as backlash from perceived inauthentic alliances or conflicts with the influencer's other affiliations. Building a relationship based on trust and mutual respect can mitigate such risks, ensuring that influencer partnerships are seen as genuine and authoritative.

As leaders seek to cultivate their digital influence, the ability to spot rising influencers before they gain widespread recognition can be a profound strategic advantage. This requires a proactive approach—monitoring trends, tracking the emergence of new voices, and engaging with upcoming influencers early in their ascendance. By doing so, leaders can foster genuine relationships and collaborations that yield long-lasting benefits for both parties.

Finally, understanding key influencers and their roles in digital power dynamics isn't a static endeavor. It demands constant vigilance, learning, and adaptation. Digital spaces are in perpetual flux, with new influencers entering and altering the landscape continuously. A thorough, ongoing assessment of who wields influence in relevant digital realms, paired with an understanding of the cultural, technological, and social shifts driving these changes, empowers leaders to remain at the forefront of influence, guiding the conversations that shape our connected world.

## Mapping Digital Networks

To understand power dynamics in the digital age, one must start by mapping the intricate networks that form the backbone of this new reality. These networks are not just a collection of connections; they're the living veins of influence pulsing through the digital landscape. In the hyperconnected world we inhabit, the notion of power has shifted from centralized hierarchies to distributed networks. Navigating these networks effectively requires a keen eye for identifying the nodes of influence and understanding how they interconnect.

In traditional power structures, influence was often concentrated in formal positions of authority. Now, digital networks have democratized influence, allowing individuals to wield power far beyond organizational boundaries. These networks transcend geographical limitations and exist on platforms where voices that might have been unheard previously can now gain attention and followers. Think of influencers, thought leaders, and even anonymous personas who command vast networks without ever stepping into a physical boardroom.

The art of mapping digital networks begins with recognizing the key players within these webs of connection. Influencers, opinion leaders, and subject matter experts often serve as hubs around which networks revolve. These are the individuals whose opinions shape conversations, alter perceptions, and inspire action. Yet, influence in digital networks doesn't equate to having the loudest voice. The true power lies in the ability to persuade, connect, and mobilize others effectively.

Leaders in the digital era must adeptly analyze these structures, understanding that individual influence can fluctuate. It's crucial to discern between noise and influence. A high follower count doesn't always translate to impactful engagement. The astute leader delves deeper, analyzing not just how many people follow a network node, but how these connections are utilized to create real-world impact.

The dynamics within digital networks are complex, driven by algorithms, social phenomena, and the human desire for connection. Leaders should seek to decode these patterns, understanding how content goes viral and the mechanisms behind information cascades. This requires both an analytical mindset and an understanding of human behavior—an intersection where data science meets psychology. Recognizing patterns can aid in predicting trends, sparking movements, and formulating strategic initiatives that resonate within these networks.

The concept of network mapping isn't new, yet its applications have evolved. A modern-day Machiavelli would argue that digital leaders must be both mapmakers and pathfinders within these extensive networks. Just as Renaissance courtiers had to navigate the intricate social structure of the courts, today's leaders must chart their course through social media channels, digital forums, and online communities. By doing so, they can identify leverage points and build authentic relationships that endure beyond transient trends.

Moreover, understanding digital networks extends to recognizing potential adversaries and competitive entities. Every action within a network can cause ripples, and leaders need to foresee the impact of their strategic moves. By visualizing these networks, identifying the connections that matter, and the influences they exert, leaders can forecast potential challenges and opportunities, creating contingency plans before friction points arise.

The pursuit of influence within these frameworks requires authenticity. In a space cluttered with content, genuine intent, and clear communication often shine brighter than mere volume. Leaders who can express their vision clearly, engage their audience, and foster two-way communication will find themselves forming stronger networks built on mutual respect and shared goals. Authentic relationships in the digital sphere are built on trust, and this trust translates into loyalty and sustained influence.

In the ever-evolving landscape of digital networks, continual reassessment and adaptation are imperative. Networks are dynamic, constantly evolving with new platforms, emerging technologies, and shifting social attitudes. A digital leader's map must be living, frequently updated to remain relevant. This requires a commitment to lifelong learning and an openness to change, embracing new paradigms and technologies as they arise.

Mapping digital networks isn't just about understanding who wields power today, but anticipating who will rise tomorrow. Leaders who cultivate a deep understanding of these networks, coupled with the ability to adapt swiftly, will harness the potential of digital influence. They'll transform complexity into competitive advantage and navigate the vast online expanse with efficacy and precision.

Ultimately, mastering the art of digital network mapping is central to understanding and thriving within the power dynamics of the digital era. It's about creating a blueprint for success that leverages the ever-changing structures of influence, allowing leaders to craft strategies that resonate across these networks and propel them toward a future of effective digital leadership. In this brave new world, those who can map and master these connections will find themselves not merely participants in the digital discourse but its very architects.

# Chapter 3:
# Building Influence in
# the Digital Age

In this hyperconnected era, where the digital realm intertwines seamlessly with real-world interactions, cultivating influence has transformed into an intricate art requiring astute navigation and strategic foresight. As Machiavelli once explored the subtleties of court politics, modern leaders now face the challenge of mastering digital platforms, where every tweet, post, and connection can ripple through networks with unpredictable momentum. Building influence here demands more than just a compelling persona; it calls for authenticity coupled with a keen understanding of social media dynamics and the power of storytelling to captivate diverse audiences. Leaders must craft their online identity with clarity and intent, knowing when to wield their presence with the subtlety of a well-placed whisper or the impact of a galvanizing proclamation. By harnessing the unparalleled reach of digital tools, astute leaders can amplify their authority, engage with communities meaningfully, and shape narratives that inspire action, all while maintaining a vigilant eye on the ever-shifting landscape of digital power dynamics. This chapter explores how to deftly navigate this landscape, ensuring influence is both enduring and ethically wielded in our evolving digital civilization.

## Crafting Your Online Persona

In the realm of digital influence, an individual's online persona serves as both their coat of arms and their primary vehicle for engaging with the world. It's not merely an extension of oneself but a carefully sculpted identity that demands diligent consideration and strategy. Crafting this persona requires recognizing the confluence of authenticity, visibility, and purpose. What others perceive you to be in the digital realm mirrors the echoes of your created narrative, underscoring the profound imprint of your virtual presence.

Authenticity remains the cornerstone of a compelling online persona. This doesn't mean simply mirroring offline traits in digital spaces. Instead, true authenticity in the digital world demands a strategic presentation of oneself that highlights one's strengths and values while resonating with the ethos of the targeted community. Here, the challenge lies in weaving together pieces of one's genuine self with the broader narrative they wish to convey. This fusion creates a persona that is not only believable but also relatable and influential.

Visibility plays a crucial role in persona crafting. In an ever-busy virtual space, simply existing isn't enough. One must stand out amidst the cacophony of voices. This doesn't always mean loud or constant oversharing. Instead, it involves crafting a narrative that consistently aligns with your core purpose while engaging with emerging trends and topics. A dynamic online presence that interacts thoughtfully with its environment will naturally draw attention and foster engagement.

Setting a clear purpose is indispensable in constructing a meaningful online persona. Without direction, individuals risk becoming just another face in the digital crowd. Leaders must align their personas with broader goals, reflecting what they stand for and what they aim to achieve. It's a strategic endeavor that involves being deliberate with content, interactions, and the overall narrative they choose to build. The primal power of storytelling can be harnessed effectively when the narrative serves a greater aim, whether it's influencing change, fostering community, or driving innovation.

Building an online persona is inherently intertwined with the notion of reputation management. Every post, interaction, and even silence contributes to how others perceive you. Today's digital leaders need to be proactive rather than reactive, anticipating not just current perceptions but future implications as well. Maintaining consistency, acknowledging mistakes, and rectifying them openly are attributes that enhance credibility and trustworthiness, key components of an influential persona.

Moreover, visual and textual branding are critical components of your online identity. The way visuals, like profile pictures and cover photos, enhance your brand narrative matters. Alongside these visuals, it's equally important how you choose your words. Language in your posts, comments, and messages should authentically reflect your voice yet align with the tonality expected by your audience. Unified branding across digital platforms ensures that your persona is instantly recognizable, reinforcing message coherence.

The platforms where you choose to engage will also shape the contours of your persona. Each digital space, whether it be professional networks like LinkedIn or more informal environments like Instagram or Twitter, offers distinct opportunities for expression and interaction. Understanding the nuances of each platform allows leaders to tailor their communication style to fit the space, maximizing influence and reach while maintaining authenticity.

Creating a successful online persona necessitates an understanding of the power dynamics at play in digital spaces. Not all voices carry equal weight, and influence is often concentrated in networks of persuasion. Identifying those key networks and engaging with them effectively can amplify your voice and reach. It's through strategic alliances and thoughtful collaborations that a digital persona enhances its standing and broadens its impact.

Another dimension to consider is adaptability. The digital world is ever-evolving, and an online persona must be agile, capable of navigating change while maintaining core values. This doesn't mean being inconsistent but rather being flexible enough to evolve with the times. Leaders who demonstrate adaptability engender respect and inspire confidence among their followers, solidifying their place as thought leaders in their field.

Privacy is another crucial aspect that cannot be overlooked. In a hyperconnected world, the balance between transparency and confidentiality defines how authentic a persona appears. Leaders need to decide what elements of their personal lives are shared without compromising professional boundaries or personal safety. Setting clear privacy parameters ensures that while your persona is open enough to build trust, it remains secure from potential digital threats.

Crafting an effective online persona also prepares leaders for potential crises and challenges. With a well-defined identity, leaders can respond more effectively to negative feedback or controversies, leveraging their established credibility to navigate through turbulent times. A resilient persona not only withstands such challenges but emerges stronger and more respected because of them.

Ultimately, the art of crafting an online persona is not static but a continually refined process. It involves introspection, strategy, and engagement with the digital landscape in a manner that fortifies one's leadership style and influence. As today's digital leaders strive to craft personas that are authentic and powerful, they make the digital age not only a space of interaction but a stage for profound influence and enduring leadership.

The journey of shaping an online persona is an empowering one, encouraging leaders to harness the full potential of digital tools to build legacies that transcend their immediate spheres of influence. By mastering the delicate art of persona crafting, leaders not only elevate their personal brand but redefine what it means to lead in the digital age.

## Leveraging Social Media for Authority

In today's hyperconnected world, the digital landscape serves as a modern arena where influence and authority are both forged and fortified. Social media, often regarded merely as a tool for connection and entertainment, holds the potential for much more—it can become the cornerstone of your strategy to establish and amplify your authority. As we explore this realm, it's crucial to acknowledge that harnessing social media for authority doesn't simply mean collecting followers and likes. It involves shaping a perception and constructing a carefully curated online persona that resonates with your audience and asserts your position of influence.

Every tweet, post, and story is not just a piece of content; it's a brick in the edifice of your digital identity. The first step in leveraging social media for authority involves a deep understanding of the platforms that are relevant to your field. While LinkedIn might be the preferred platform for B2B leaders, Instagram's visual storytelling capability is invaluable for influencers in fashion, art, or lifestyle. Similarly, TikTok's rapid rise offers untapped potential for those who can turn creativity into engagement. Knowing these nuances helps strategize your approach, ensuring you're not just heard, but remembered.

Establishing authority also means becoming a consistent and reliable source of valuable content. Think of yourself as a cultivator of knowledge and expertise in your field, crafting content that educates, enlightens, or even entertains, but always aligns with your overarching message. Create a mosaic of insights, personal anecdotes, and industry updates that paints you as an erudite leader. Within this tapestry, authenticity is your strongest thread. Audiences today crave genuine connections over manufactured personas. This authenticity fosters trust, which is foundational to influence.

*Consider this:* authority isn't conferred merely by expertise alone—it demands social proof. Social proof, when utilized effectively, acts as a multiplier for your influence. Engage with other influential figures, participate in digital dialogues, and contribute to conversations that showcase your thought leadership. The endorsements you receive, the collaborative projects, and even constructive challenges to your ideas enrich your public profile, affirming your position within your network.

Moreover, leveraging social media for authority means embracing the role of an active participant in the community you've chosen. Engage with your audience by responding to comments, asking for feedback, and being approachable. This interaction fosters a sense of community and trust, transforming passive followers into active advocates. Remember, every interaction is an opportunity to demonstrate humility and openness, inviting deeper conversations and more meaningful connections.

Amidst the sea of content, standing out requires creativity and adaptability. Experimentation is key—try varied formats like live videos, podcasts, and interactive sessions to keep your audience engaged. Each format offers unique ways to showcase your expertise and connect on a deeper level. However, never lose sight of the data. Utilize analytics tools to gauge what resonates, and refine your strategies accordingly. This flexible, data-driven approach ensures you remain relevant and authoritative amidst ever-evolving digital dynamics.

Persistence and consistency cannot be overstated in the quest for authority. In our fast-paced digital age, authority isn't built overnight. It is a deliberate process, requiring consistent nurturing and engagement. Dedicate time to plan, execute, and evaluate your social media strategy. Repetition of your core message across different mediums and moments ensures it's internalized by your audience, culminating in a lasting impression.

Yet, the quest for digital authority through social media also demands strategic humility. It's essential to acknowledge when a particular course of action or content type doesn't yield the desired results. Be prepared to pivot, to continuously learn from both successes and setbacks. This adaptability not only maintains your relevance but also demonstrates resilience, a trait people intuitively respect and gravitate towards.

As we've touched upon the indispensable role of social media in crafting authority, it's important to envisage a broader perspective. Your online demeanor should reflect not just your expertise but also your values and vision. Social media isn't just about showcasing capability; it's an avenue to communicate what you stand for as a leader. This alignment between your message and your mission enhances authenticity, nurturing a credible, compelling narrative in the minds of your audience.

Ultimately, the true power of leveraging social media for authority lies in its ability to transcend mere digital interaction, leading to tangible influence in the real world. By strategically positioning yourself as an authoritative voice in your domain, social media can be the megaphone that amplifies your ideas beyond geographical and traditional constraints, crafting not just an audience, but a community of advocates who propel your leadership from the screens to the tangible realms of influence and impact.

# Chapter 4:
## The Art of Modern Persuasion

In the labyrinth of today's digital world, mastering the art of persuasion requires more than just eloquence; it demands a nuanced understanding of virtual landscapes and the skill to navigate them. With every interaction, leaders must craft messages that not only resonate but also inspire and motivate across diverse platforms. It's about harnessing the power of digital communication to build genuine trust, even when eyes never meet. Central to modern persuasion is the ability to adapt strategies to suit rapidly shifting contexts, using empathy and insight to engage an increasingly skeptical audience. Authenticity becomes the currency with which influence is built, with leaders needing to balance the fine line between personal branding and genuine connection. By leveraging data and storytelling in their communications, they'll anchor their leadership in credibility, making themselves heard above the cacophony of digital noise. It's an art, certainly—one where the brush strokes of intention, genuineness, and foresight paint the path to enduring influence.

## Strategies for Effective Communication

In a world where screens dominate our interactions, the art of communication has transformed profoundly. The digital age presents both challenges and opportunities; hence, modern leaders must master communication strategies that resonate across diverse platforms and audiences. At the center of effective communication lies the ability to be both articulate and relatable, merging traditional persuasion techniques with the adaptability of modern technology.

Firstly, grasping the power of storytelling is essential. Narratives have an age-old appeal, tapping into emotions and making messages memorable. In today's fast-paced world, the most effective leaders weave stories into their communication, ensuring that their messages are not only understood but felt. This requires a deep understanding of one's audience and the cultural nuances that influence perception.

Furthermore, the brevity and clarity of your message can amplify its impact. The digital landscape is saturated with information, making it crucial to cut through the noise. Leaders are tasked with crafting messages that are concise yet impactful; every word must serve a purpose. This skill is less about saying less and more about saying what truly matters in a way that's easily digestible.

Personalization has emerged as a key strategy in effective communication. In an era where algorithms tailor our digital experiences, there is an expectation for personalized interactions. Leaders should leverage this by addressing individual needs and concerns, whether through personalized emails, social media interactions, or direct messages. This fosters a sense of connection and relevance that is hard to achieve in one-size-fits-all communication.

Moreover, building an authentic voice is vital. Authenticity cultivates trust—a cornerstone of influence.

Today's leaders must be genuine and transparent, showcasing their values and beliefs through their words and actions. This doesn't mean oversharing but finding a balance between professional integrity and personal expression. Authentic communication is relatable and engenders loyalty among audiences.

Digital communication also calls for strategic use of multimedia tools. From video and podcasts to infographics and live streams, leveraging various media can enhance engagement. These tools can make messages more accessible, catering to diverse learning styles and preferences. It's about selecting the right medium to convey the message effectively while maintaining the audience's interest.

Incorporating feedback loops in communication strategies can't be overemphasized. Encouraging dialogue and listening to responses allows leaders to adapt and refine their messages as necessary. Whether through comments on social media or direct feedback from team members, this input is invaluable. It empowers leaders to address concerns promptly, demonstrating that they value and consider diverse perspectives.

Another powerful strategy is practicing active listening. Truly understanding others requires undivided attention and empathy. Leaders should aim to listen not just to respond but to understand and integrate feedback into decision-making. Active listening fosters deeper connections and showcases respect for others' viewpoints, crucial traits in building strong relationships.

The ability to adapt messaging across platforms is equally important. Different digital platforms have distinct audiences and protocols. A message on LinkedIn should maintain professionalism, whereas a message on Instagram might be more visual and informal. Leaders need to tailor their communication style to fit the platform while maintaining their core message and values.

Moreover, in an era where misinformation can spread like wildfire, credibility and fact-checking are paramount. Leaders must ensure their messages are based on verified information, establishing themselves as reliable sources. This strengthens their credibility and the effectiveness of their communication. Mitigating the spread of misinformation should be an active part of a leader's communication strategy.

Finally, employing emotional intelligence in communication can significantly enhance a leader's influence. Understanding and navigating emotions—both theirs and others'—allows leaders to connect on a deeper, more human level. Emotional intelligence helps in articulating messages that resonate emotionally while also managing challenging feedback or conflicts with tact.

In conclusion, strategies for effective communication in the digital age involve a blend of timeless persuasion tactics and modern technological tools. Leaders must be storytellers, active listeners, and adapt their messages to fit the nuances of each platform. Through authenticity, personalization, and emotional intelligence, leaders can craft communication strategies that resonate deeply and empower them to lead in a hyperconnected world. By mastering these strategies, leaders can navigate the complexities of modern leadership, ensuring their influence is not only felt but remembered.

## Building Trust in a Virtual World

The foundation of any persuasive effort is trust. In a virtual world, establishing trust isn't just challenging, it's a nuanced art form. Trust, once a commodity exchanged face-to-face, now bears the complexity of a thousand digital interactions. As leaders, understanding how trust plays out online becomes essential, but how do you authentically build it when eye contact and handshakes are out of the equation?

Consider credibility your first port of call. Establishing credibility in a digital space often starts with your online persona—crafted with precision and authenticity. Don't just portray an image; embody it with consistency. An inconsistency between words and actions, no matter how minute, can erode trust more swiftly than you'd think. It's about the reliability in the delivery of your promises, however big or small. If you're perceived as someone who delivers what they pledge, you've laid the cornerstone for trust.

Building relationships in a virtual world requires continuous effort and presence. Some may argue that virtual interactions lack the warmth of physical meetings. While there may be some truth to that, it's the emotional resonance that counts. This means being real—responding timely, showing empathy, and engaging with sincerity. Your virtual engagements should resonate with the understanding that there's a person behind the screen, rather than just a task to be accomplished.

*Effective communication* is the linchpin in building trust. Without the benefit of physical presence, our words and tone carry even greater weight. Express thoughts clearly, avoid misunderstandings, and actively listen to those on the other side of the screen. Remember, in the absence of physical cues, words become your most powerful ally. They must be chosen wisely, with a focus not just on clarity but on transparency, which in itself is a powerful trust-builder.

Transparency leads us directly to the concept of authenticity. In a world where digital personas can be meticulously curated, authenticity stands out as a beacon of trust. Authentic leaders are unafraid to show vulnerability. They share not only their successes but their challenges and failures. This openness invites connection and fosters faithfulness—even in an online setting. Authenticity is about being honest in your intentions and actions, about being relatable, and, above all, about building a genuine connection that transcends digital barriers.

Moreover, fostering trust also requires a commitment to security and privacy. In today's digital age, where breaches are a common fear, security isn't just a technical concern but a trust issue. Ensuring secure communication channels and protecting personal information are critical steps in fostering a sense of safety and reliability. People are more likely to trust and engage when they feel their data is protected and valued.

Engagement is never a one-way street. For trust to become a mutual affair, encourage feedback and act on it. Virtual environments offer abundant opportunities for feedback loops. Social media, emails, and forums allow for real-time interaction. Prompt responses, active problem-solving, and visible changes in response to feedback create an atmosphere where trust can thrive.

The digital world is vast and filled with noise. Distinguishing yourself and building trust involves creating value through thought leadership. Leveraging platforms to share valuable insights and fostering dialogues positions you as an authority. This authority must be grounded in consistency and relevance, aligning your message with audience needs and expectations.

Digital trust, however, also requires patience and resilience. Unlike face-to-face interactions, where trust might be quickly forged over common interests, building trust online can take time. It requires the perseverance to consistently show up—being present in the digital conversations and value streams that matter. Trust doesn't happen overnight, but rather develops as others observe a continuous alignment of intention and action.

**Mentorship and guidance** further extend opportunities for establishing trust. Offering guidance, sharing experiences, and advising others helps position you as a dependable figure within a virtual community. As more people begin to respect your insights and advice, the web of trust strengthens, pulling others into a communal sense of reliability and faith.

Adapting Machiavelli's lessons to this digital landscape calls for an understanding of the subtleties of trust—knowing when to extend it, how to reciprocate it, and the wisdom to protect it. It involves the orchestration of digital presence, perception, security, and interpersonal engagements, all in harmony with one another.

Among all these strategies, remember that trust in a virtual world is an ongoing pursuit. The landscape of technology may change, but the human need for connection and trust remains a constant. By ensuring that every digital footprint you create is marked by transparency, authenticity, and reliability, you don't just build influence—you're crafting a trusted presence, critical in the art of modern persuasion. This presence is what will guide and define your legacy as a leader in an ever-evolving digital arena.

# Chapter 5:
# Decision-Making in the Age
# of Information Overload

In the digital age, leaders face the Herculean task of sifting through a deluge of information, transforming the chaos into clarity for effective decision-making. The abundance of data, while a treasure trove of insights, presents a paradox; it offers both opportunity and overwhelming complexity. Leaders must now possess the agility to swiftly navigate these data streams, discerning pertinent facts from noise, and fine-tuning their instinct for strategic foresight. This era demands a harmonious balance between speed and precision, where decisions must be informed by data yet not paralyzed by over-analysis. Harnessing the art of discernment, today's leaders can channel Machiavellian wisdom into actionable intelligence, ensuring that each choice aligns with broader strategic objectives while embracing the nuances of a hyperconnected world. In this intricate dance of data and intuition, decision-making becomes not just a skill but an art form, guiding digital leaders to thrive amidst information overload.

## Navigating Data-Driven Decisions

In an era characterized by the relentless surge of information, modern leaders face the monumental challenge of navigating data-driven decisions. The ceaseless flow of data presents both an opportunity and a conundrum. With every click, swipe, and digital interaction leaving behind a footprint, leaders are equipped with unprecedented insights into behaviors, preferences, and trends. However, the sheer volume of data can easily become overwhelming, clouding the clarity needed for effective decision-making.

Being data-driven in decision-making is not merely about possessing data; it's about mastering the ability to sift through the noise to extract meaningful insights. Modern leaders, much like seasoned oracles, must interpret these insights to predict outcomes and orchestrate informed strategies. They need to balance quantitative data with qualitative insights, intuition with analysis, and immediate needs with long-term objectives. These challenges demand a harmonious blend of analytical prowess and strategic foresight, akin to wielding both sword and shield in digital warfare.

The speed at which decisions need to be made in today's digital landscape is another factor that compounds the complexity. In previous eras, leaders might have had the luxury of time to deliberate. Today, the lag between action and consequence has narrowed significantly, necessitating swifter decision-making processes. Those who hesitate risk missing pivotal opportunities or, worse, facing irreversible consequences. This dynamic environment favors leaders who can act decisively yet draw wisdom from their data resources.

Modern tools and technologies have aimed to alleviate some of these pressures by enhancing leaders' capabilities to process vast amounts of information swiftly. Machine learning algorithms and artificial intelligence play critical roles in transforming raw data into actionable insights. They help in identifying patterns that would otherwise remain hidden, providing clarity amidst complexity. Yet, it is the leader's responsibility to critically assess these algorithm-generated insights, ensuring that they align with human-centric values and organizational goals.

Integrating these technological insights into strategic planning presents its own set of challenges. It's not enough to collect data; leaders must ask the right questions to harness data's full potential. What are the underlying trends that the data reveals? How do these insights align with the broader mission and vision of the organization? What potential biases might skew these analytics? Such questions ensure that data-driven decisions are not only tactical but also ethical and sustainable.

In the digital age, the proverbial "gut feeling" still holds value alongside hard data. Intuition, sharpened by experience, acts as the critical complement to data analysis. It guides leaders in recognizing moments when data may be misleading or when human sentiment defies analytical predictions. The art lies in knowing when to trust data-driven insights and when to heed the wisdom accrued through years of leadership experience.

Critical to this process is the establishment of a robust data-driven culture within an organization. A culture that empowers individuals at all levels to contribute to decision-making not only democratizes insights but enriches the decision-making process itself. This inclusivity ensures diverse perspectives are accounted for, mitigating the risk of echo chambers and fostering innovation. Leaders must, therefore, not only utilize data themselves but encourage a data-first mindset throughout the organization.

Navigating data-driven decisions also involves understanding the implications of those decisions on human and organizational dynamics. Leaders today must be adept in considering how decisions influence team morale, customer relationships, and stakeholder trust. It's about finding that delicate balance where data enhances human interactions without overshadowing the inherently human elements of empathy and connection.

The journey to mastering data-driven decisions is iterative, demanding a commitment to continuous learning and adaptation. Technological advancements continuously reshape the data landscape, introducing new tools and methodologies that leaders must stay abreast of. As they do so, they build resilience against decision fatigue, developing the agility to pivot strategies in response to emerging digital trends and disruptions.

In conclusion, the art of navigating data-driven decisions is a dynamic interplay of technology, intuition, ethics, and foresight. Propelled by data, today's leaders must wield it with the skill akin to a maestro conducting an orchestra—balancing precision with creativity, vision with action, and analytics with empathy. By mastering these competencies, they position themselves to lead effectively and ethically in the age of information overload.

## Balancing Speed and Accuracy

In this era of rapid technological advancement, leaders often find themselves bombarded by an avalanche of information. The sheer volume of data available today can be both a blessing and a curse. On one hand, access to a wealth of information can empower leaders to make well-informed, strategic decisions. On the other hand, it can lead to paralysis by analysis, where sifting through data becomes an overwhelming task, delaying critical decisions. This brings us to the quintessential challenge: balancing speed with accuracy.

Speed, in decision-making, is crucial in a world where market dynamics and technological landscapes shift with the blink of an eye. Yet, speed without purpose can be reckless. Decisions made too hastily, without adequate analysis, risk jeopardizing the very objectives they aim to achieve. Conversely, an excessive focus on accuracy can transform decision-making into an endless quest for perfection, stalling progress when timely action is needed most.

Modern leaders must strive to develop an instinct akin to that of a seasoned chess player, one who can think several moves ahead but also recognize when it's time to act decisively. This balancing act requires not only intellectual agility but also a keen sense of prioritization—knowing which decisions warrant deep exploration and which can be expedited based on trustworthy heuristics or experience.

Four centuries ago, Niccolò Machiavelli emphasized the importance of adapting to the times. In today's digital age, this means embracing data-driven insights while remaining agile. Leaders must cultivate a mindset that embraces both the art and science of decision-making, understanding when to rely on data and when to trust their gut. Such a mindset is cultivated through continual learning and experience, informed by both successes and failures.

The deluge of information at our fingertips necessitates the use of sophisticated technologies for processing and analyzing data. Artificial intelligence and machine learning algorithms are indispensable tools for modern leaders seeking to streamline decision-making processes. These technologies can sift through vast datasets to uncover patterns, providing leaders with distilled insights that might otherwise remain hidden amidst a digital clutter.

However, the reliance on technology should never overshadow the human element of decision-making. Algorithms, while powerful, operate based on predefined rules, and are subject to biases inherent in their programming. Human intuition and empathy play pivotal roles in contextualizing data, ensuring that decisions remain aligned with human values and ethical standards.

Another critical strategy for balancing speed with accuracy involves fostering a culture of collaboration within leadership environments. Diverse teams can harness a range of perspectives, leading to more comprehensive evaluations of the issues at hand. By leveraging the collective intelligence of their teams, leaders can expedite decision-making without compromising on the depth of analysis. Cross-disciplinary collaboration, facilitated by digital tools and platforms, becomes an invaluable asset.

It's essential for leaders to establish a clear framework for decision-making. This involves delineating which types of decisions require rigorous data analysis and which can be made more intuitively. Setting these parameters helps prevent decision-making from becoming an endless endeavor, fraught with indecision. It allows leaders to act with confidence, even when time is of the essence.

Developing a keen understanding of risk tolerance is also vital in balancing speed and accuracy. Leaders need to recognize the stakes involved in each decision and assess their risk appetite accordingly. In some scenarios, being first to market with a good-enough solution trumps delaying for perfect accuracy. In others, a slight miscalculation could have significant ramifications, necessitating a more cautious approach.

In high-stakes environments, the ability to pivot swiftly is just as important as making the initial decision. Implementing a feedback loop to monitor outcomes allows leaders to refine their strategies in real-time, adapting to new information as it becomes available. This adaptive approach ensures resilience and agility, key traits in sustaining competitive advantage over time.

The need for speed in decision-making often causes stress, especially in a hyperconnected world where expectations for immediacy are ever-present. Leaders must also consider the impact their decision-making style has on their teams. A culture that equates speed with success can lead to burnout, undermining long-term performance. Therefore, it is crucial for leaders to instill work practices that emphasize sustainable productivity and mental well-being, reinforcing that precision and prudence are as valued as swiftness.

Finally, learning from past decisions—both successful and otherwise—offers valuable insights for future decision-making. By reflecting on what worked and what didn't, leaders can better hone their instinctive decision-making abilities, refining their process of balancing speed and accuracy. This continual evolution is integral to mastering the art of leadership in the age of information overload.

In sum, the equilibrium between speed and accuracy doesn't exist in rigidity but in adaptability. Today's leaders must cultivate a dynamic approach, one that leverages both data and instinct, foresight and hindsight. By doing so, they can make impactful decisions that propel them forward in an ever-accelerating digital landscape.

# Chapter 6:
## Navigating Ethical Challenges

In an era where the digital landscape transforms with breathtaking speed, modern leaders face ethical challenges that demand agility and foresight. At the heart of this digital revolution lies the delicate balance between innovation and accountability. Leaders must navigate an intricate web of privacy concerns, ensuring transparency while grappling with the dual imperatives of profit and ethics. It's about making choices that respect individual rights and stakeholder interests without compromising business growth. The path ahead requires leaders not just to adapt, but to carve a new ethical blueprint that aligns with the rapidly evolving technological norms. As they steer through this complexity, embracing a proactive stance on ethical dilemmas can turn potential pitfalls into opportunities for trust-building and long-term sustainability. The keys to mastering these challenges lie in foresight, integrity, and the courage to stand firm in values while riding the waves of digital transformation.

## Privacy Concerns and Transparency

In an age where almost every action leaves a digital footprint, privacy has become a pivotal concern for leaders striving to ethically harness the power of technology. Modern leaders need to be acutely aware of how personal and organizational data is collected, used, and potentially weaponized. Transparency is not just an ethical obligation but a strategic necessity in building trust and maintaining integrity in digital spaces.

Where once the lines between public and private were clearly delineated, the digital revolution has blurred those boundaries. The influx of data, generated by everything from social media interactions to mobile device sensors, offers leaders a treasure trove of information. Yet, this treasure is fraught with peril. Missteps in data management can lead to breaches of trust that are harder to repair than ever before. Leaders must vigilantly ensure that the use of personal data respects privacy rights, and they must communicate these commitments clearly.

Consider the implications of a leader's actions in a world connected by technology. While it's tempting to wield power through the lens of all-seeing data analytics, the potential for abuse is significant. Leaders must ask themselves not just what can be done with available data but what should be done, guiding decision-making with a Machiavellian wisdom tempered by modern ethical standards.

Transparency serves as the cornerstone for managing privacy concerns. By being open about data collection practices, leaders can foster a culture of trust and accountability. This transparency is essential for aligning with both regulatory standards and the ethical expectations of stakeholders. The challenge lies not only in the 'what' of transparency—detailing what data is collected and how it is used—but also in the 'why.' Leaders must articulate a compelling reason for their data practices that resonates with the values of those they serve.

As regulatory landscapes evolve, compliance with laws such as the General Data Protection Regulation (GDPR) and the California Consumer Privacy Act (CCPA) becomes vital. Yet, legislative adherence is merely the starting point. True mastery of digital leadership in respect to privacy concerns involves going beyond what is mandated, embedding transparency into the very fabric of organizational culture.

The practice of transparency requires continuous engagement and innovation. It's not enough to merely declare data policies; leaders must also ensure that these policies are accessible and understandable. This calls for clear, jargon-free communication that empowers individuals to make informed choices about their shared data. In this way, transparency becomes an exercise in partnership rather than a unilateral declaration, a signal that leaders value and respect their stakeholders' privacy.

However, balancing transparency with the need to maintain competitive advantage requires deft maneuvering. Intellectual property, proprietary algorithms, and business strategies often hinge on controlled access to information. Here, transparency is about finding the equilibrium between openness and confidentiality, ensuring that the organization's integrity remains intact without reneging on ethical commitments to privacy.

The stakes are exceptionally high. Breaches of trust can precipitate not just a loss of reputation but also significant financial and legal repercussions. Today's hyperconnected world means that news of indiscretions spreads rapidly, potentially inciting public backlash and eroding the social capital that leaders have painstakingly built over time. Thus, establishing a robust framework for privacy protection isn't just an ethical imperative but a strategic one.

In this context, leading by example is paramount. Leaders who visibly prioritize privacy through their actions and decisions set a tone that permeates through the organization. Their commitment can inspire others to value and protect privacy, creating a ripple effect that strengthens the organization's ethical foundation.

Furthermore, ethical leadership demands a proactive approach to potential privacy breaches. Establishing protocols for handling data breaches with transparency ensures stakeholders are informed and can trust the organization to act swiftly and responsibly. This involves preparing in advance— having communication plans and channels ready to mitigate damage and demonstrate accountability should a breach occur.

Ultimately, navigating privacy concerns and transparency isn't a finite task—it's an ongoing dialogue. Leaders must remain adaptable and responsive to the evolving technological and regulatory environment while continuously seeking ways to enhance their strategies. This conversation requires the involvement of diverse voices within the organization and beyond, incorporating perspectives that might otherwise be overlooked.

In conclusion, privacy concerns and transparency are intertwined with the very essence of digital leadership. By centering these principles, modern leaders can redefine influence and authority in a way that respects individual rights and builds enduring success. In this digital age, where boundaries and borders are constantly tested, it's the adherence to ethical transparency that will distinguish those who lead effectively from those who falter. In channeling Machiavellian foresight into these modern challenges, leaders can wield their influence not merely for power but for meaningful, responsible impact.

## Balancing Profit and Ethics

In the relentless pursuit of success, where the bottom line often stands as the ultimate measure, balancing profit and ethics becomes a formidable challenge. Leaders today find themselves in a world that not only demands profitability but also places a significant emphasis on ethical governance. This balance is not just about doing what's legal; it's about doing what's right, and therein lies the complexity.

In many ways, the digital age has intensified the scrutiny on leadership decisions. Information flows at an unprecedented speed, and leaders are now under the microscope. Every choice, whether it involves data privacy, environmental sustainability, or employee welfare, can instantly become public knowledge. This transparency demands a new kind of leadership—one that seamlessly integrates ethical considerations into every decision.

But how can leaders strike this delicate balance? It starts by understanding that ethics and profit are not mutually exclusive. In fact, aligning business goals with ethical practices can often lead to stronger, more sustainable profits. This alignment requires a shift in perspective, a realization that ethical practices contribute to brand value, customer loyalty, and employee satisfaction. Such an integration is no longer a luxury but a necessity.

Consider, for instance, the growing consumer demand for transparency. Today's consumers are more informed and empowered than ever before. They expect clarity on how products are sourced, how employees are treated, and how companies contribute to societal goals. A company that openly shares its ethical practices builds trust, creating a loyal customer base that can sustain profitability.

Similarly, in the realm of employee management, ethics play a crucial role. Modern employees are seeking more than just a paycheck; they're looking for workplaces that reflect their values. Companies that foster inclusive, empowering environments often witness lower turnover rates and heightened productivity, factors that directly contribute to profitability.

Of course, the path to ethical profitability is fraught with challenges. The temptation to cut corners for short-term gains can be overwhelming, especially in competitive markets. Leaders are often caught in a tug-of-war between investor expectations and ethical responsibilities. Navigating this requires not only a moral compass but also strategic foresight.

This foresight involves anticipating the long-term consequences of decisions. Leaders must continuously assess how their choices today will shape their brand's reputation and societal impact tomorrow. Ethical missteps can lead to substantial financial penalties and irrevocable damage to the company's reputation, eroding consumer trust and market position.

The digital era also introduces unique ethical dilemmas, particularly in the realm of data usage. With massive amounts of consumer data at their fingertips, companies have the power to drive personalized marketing, improve services, and anticipate consumer needs. Yet, this power comes with significant responsibility. Misusing data can lead to breaches of privacy, triggering scandals that not only harm individuals but also tarnish the company's integrity.

To navigate these challenges, leaders must cultivate an ethical culture within their organizations. This involves creating robust policies that prioritize ethical considerations in decision-making processes. Training programs, ethical guidelines, and a clear framework for accountability are essential tools in fostering such a culture. Empathy and open dialogue should be encouraged, ensuring that every team member understands their role in the ethical narrative of the company.

Moreover, leaders must lead by example. Ethical leadership is contagious—as leaders demonstrate integrity in their actions, they inspire their teams to follow suit. This approach not only cement ethical practices but also fortifies the organization's reputation from the ground up.

The digital landscape, while adding complexity, also offers opportunities to reinforce ethical standards. Advanced technologies can be harnessed to ensure transparency and accountability in ways previously unimaginable. Blockchain, for example, provides immutable records that can validate ethical claims about product sourcing or fair labor practices. Similarly, AI can enhance compliance by monitoring and flagging unethical activities before they escalate into significant issues.

In the end, navigating the intersection of profit and ethics requires a steadfast commitment to principles and an adaptive strategy that aligns with the evolving digital environment. As Machiavelli suggested, leaders must understand and foresee changes. In today's context, this means adapting ethical frameworks to leverage technology responsibly, all while maintaining a focus on those timeless principles of honesty and social responsibility.

Leaders who master this balance not only lead companies to financial success but also contribute positively to society—crafting a legacy that stands the test of time. In the digital age, where influence can be as fleeting as a viral tweet, it is this steadfast ethical commitment that anchors true leadership, assuring that profits gained are not at the expense of our shared future but in service of it.

Thus, the challenge and beauty of balancing profit and ethics in the digital age lies in the harmonization of values—where prosperity and integrity are interwoven, creating a tapestry that reflects the best of humanity in an era defined by exponential change and infinite connectivity.

# Chapter 7:
## Establishing Authority in Hyperconnected Environments

In today's hyperconnected world, establishing authority requires a strategic blend of authenticity, agility, and relentless engagement across digital platforms. The key lies in understanding that the digital sphere amplifies voices and democratizes influence, altering traditional power dynamics. To command respect and attention, modern leaders must not only craft a compelling narrative but also actively participate in diverse digital ecosystems—echoing Machiavelli's notion of adapting to the times. This isn't about wielding authority from a distance; it's about establishing a presence that feels both approachable and dynamic, grounded in real-time interactions. By managing online reputations with precision and leveraging digital channels effectively, leaders can build a perception of authority that resonates with authenticity and transparency. Remaining adaptable and responsive in this ever-evolving landscape is crucial. Those who master this will not merely survive today's whirlwind of connectivity—they will thrive, guiding their followers with confidence and clarity through the noise of the digital age, turning hyperconnectivity from a challenge into an unrivaled advantage.

## Commanding Attention Through Digital Channels

In our hyperconnected world, where information flows at the speed of light, capturing and maintaining attention is the currency of authority. The digital landscape is vast and diverse, but at its core lies a fundamental human desire: connection. To command attention through digital channels, leaders must first understand this intrinsic need, crafting messages and strategies that resonate deeply with their audiences. Success in this arena isn't just about being seen but about being felt and understood. The challenge and opportunity for modern leaders are to harness these echo chambers of influence for the greater good.

Historically, authority was embodied by physical presence and charisma. Today, the arena has shifted to screens and streams, where influence can be wielded by those who adapt quickly and efficiently. The task of commanding attention online is akin to orchestrating a symphony; it requires timing, precision, and a deep understanding of the instruments at your disposal. Platforms such as social media, blogs, and digital forums are the concert halls of the 21st century. To leverage them effectively, leaders must craft compelling narratives that cut through the noise and engage the audience on an emotional level.

Storytelling remains one of the most potent tools in this digital arsenal. Great stories transcend time and platforms; they resonate because they're relatable and often convey universal truths. Crafting a story in today's digital era involves more than just the narrative itself—it's about the presentation, the engagement, and the interaction with the audience. This is where leaders must be both artists and technicians, knowing which mediums to use and how to deploy content for maximum impact. Whether through a well-timed tweet or a captivating video, every piece of content is an opportunity to connect authentically with your audience.

However, commanding attention isn't just about creating content; it's about positioning yourself as a thought leader — an entity around which conversations naturally gravitate. To do this, consistency and credibility are key. Leaders must be habitual with their messaging, maintaining a steady stream of communication that reinforces their core values and vision. This involves a strategic understanding of the digital landscape, knowing when and where to place messages to achieve the desired impact.

Another crucial aspect of commanding attention lies in understanding the algorithms that govern digital platforms. These algorithms determine visibility, making them powerful gatekeepers of attention. By mastering these algorithms, leaders can tilt the scales of attention in their favor, ensuring their messages reach the intended audience. Engaging with analytics and feedback in a continuous loop allows leaders to refine their approach, ensuring relevance and resonance.

But why is commanding attention so important? At its core, attention is the first step towards influence. In a world overwhelmed with choices and messages, gaining that initial interest opens a doorway to deeper engagement. Leaders who can capture and hold attention are better positioned to drive change, influence opinions, and inspire action. Indeed, effective digital leaders understand that sustained attention stems not just from the content itself, but from the values and authenticity behind it.

Furthermore, the digital ecosystem thrives on interaction. The most successful leaders are those who foster engaging communities around their brand or message. This involves not just broadcasting information but actively listening and responding. Community management becomes a dance of dialogue and diplomacy, where leaders can demonstrate empathy and authenticity. Through these interactions, leaders build trust—a cornerstone of authority in any era.

In commanding attention, it's also pivotal for leaders to understand and adapt to the ever-shifting digital zeitgeist. Internet culture evolves rapidly, shaped by memes, viral trends, and societal shifts. Leaders must be agile enough to pivot their messaging to remain relevant without compromising their core principles. This requires an ongoing commitment to learning and adapting, staying plugged into the current cultural undercurrents.

For those who master the art of commanding attention, the rewards can be profound. They can shape narratives, influence public discourse, and drive societal change. In a digital landscape where every voice has the potential to echo across the globe, those with the skills to capture and direct attention wield unparalleled power. But with great power comes great responsibility; leaders must wield this power ethically, ensuring their messages contribute positively to the digital dialogue.

In summary, commanding attention through digital channels is both an art and a science. It requires a blend of storytelling, strategic positioning, technical acumen, and cultural awareness. Modern leaders who wish to establish authority in these hyperconnected environments must embrace these elements, understanding that true authority comes not from controlling the narrative but from engaging with it. The digital stage awaits those bold enough to step into the spotlight and brave enough to handle the echoes of their influence.

## Managing Online Reputations

In the age of hyperconnectivity, managing one's online reputation is akin to safeguarding a critical asset. For modern leaders, the digital realm offers immense opportunities to establish authority, yet it also presents pitfalls that can undermine this authority in an instant. The path to mastering online reputation management is paved with discernment, adaptability, and a deep understanding of the digital narratives shaping public perceptions.

At the heart of managing online reputations is the imperative to maintain consistent and authentic digital personas. Online, your persona is often the first, and sometimes the only, impression others will get. Authenticity in digital communications is crucial; it's not merely about projecting an image but embodying that image in every nuance of online interaction. Leaders must align their digital personas with their values and mission to cultivate trust among audiences.

Furthermore, the art of managing an online reputation requires vigilance and agility. The digital world moves at a relentless pace, and the tides of opinion can shift rapidly. Leaders must not only monitor what is being said about them but also engage proactively with feedback. Instead of shying away from criticism or dissent, they should view these as opportunities to learn and address legitimate concerns. This engagement reflects strength and leadership, ultimately enhancing credibility.

Engagement, however, must be strategic. It isn't merely about responding to every comment or post but rather focusing on interactions that offer meaningful opportunities to connect or clarify. Leaders can implement listening tools to track mentions, measure sentiment, and identify trends that might influence public perception. In this regard, data analytics becomes a powerful ally, providing insights into audience behavior and highlighting shifts in sentiment that may require swift action.

In this dynamic landscape, it is also essential to cultivate a sense of community around your digital presence. Building a community means more than amassing followers; it involves nurturing an ecosystem where dialogue is encouraged, and relationships are fostered. A robust digital community can act as a buffer and a beacon, defending against unwarranted criticism and amplifying positive narratives. Loyalty built through these interactions can solidify a leader's standing, even when challenges arise.

Another pillar of managing online reputations is storytelling. Stories have a unique power to humanize brands and leaders alike, transforming abstract concepts into relatable narratives. By sharing stories that reflect personal journeys, triumphs, and even failures, leaders can craft compelling narratives that resonate with their audience. This narrative approach offers transparency and personal connection, which are instrumental in building and maintaining trust.

Then there is the unavoidable fact of digital permanence. The internet never forgets, and actions or statements made online can have lasting implications. Leaders must be judicious with the content they create and endorse, considering the long-term implications of their digital footprint. This requires foresight and, often, consultation with trusted advisors to ensure that their digital narrative aligns with their evolving personal and professional journeys.

In managing online reputations, leaders should not overlook the potential of collaborations to bolster reputation. Partnering with respected figures or aligning with reputable causes can extend influence and affirm authority. These collaborations should be authentic and align with the leader's values, ensuring coherence in how the leader's digital persona is perceived across different audiences and sectors.

Finally, while managing one's online reputation, it is vital to prepare for crises. Leaders should have contingency plans in place to address potential reputation threats swiftly and effectively. These plans should include clear communication strategies that detail how to address misinformation or negative press, ensuring that the leader's response is timely and resonates with transparency and accountability.

The hyperconnected world demands a Machiavellian dexterity in managing online reputations. To cultivate authority in this space, leaders need to balance authenticity with strategic engagement, employ tools to gain insights, nurture communities, and harness the power of narratives. It is a comprehensive commitment to navigating the complexities of the digital realm, translating challenges into opportunities for growth and influence.

Success in managing online reputations is not about avoiding missteps altogether but demonstrating resilience and adaptability when they occur. Through learning and evolving with the digital landscape, leaders can engrain their authority, leaving an enduring legacy. This mastery of digital reputation management, while rooted in historic principles, is definitively forward-looking, preparing leaders to thrive in the unpredictable currents of today's digital world.

# Chapter 8:
## Crisis Management in Real Time

In an era where digital landscapes shift at lightning speed, modern leaders must respond adeptly to crises that emerge without warning, leveraging Machiavellian acumen for swift and strategic action. The digital realm's interconnectedness means that backlash can amplify quickly, demanding real-time responses that are both decisive and empathetic. Leaders who master crisis management possess the ability to turn potential disasters into opportunities for resilience and growth. By developing robust strategies for digital resilience, such leaders can maintain equilibrium in the face of adversity, preserving trust and authority. This requires not only the anticipation of diverse scenarios but also the cultivation of an agile mindset—ready to pivot under pressure. Navigating crises in real time is less about thwarting every digital tempest and more about knowing when and how to anchor core values while staying nimble amidst chaos. Thus, resilience in today's hyperconnected world is crafted through the art of balancing immediacy with strategic foresight, ensuring that leadership remains steadfast even when the digital waves roar.

## Responding to Digital Backlashes

In today's hyperconnected digital landscape, information spreads at the speed of light, amplifying both praise and criticism. For modern leaders, understanding the art of crisis management isn't just advantageous; it's essential. Just like in Machiavelli's time, the stakes are high, and the court of public opinion can make or break reputations almost instantaneously. In this realm, digital backlashes loom as formidable challenges, requiring not just reactive strategies but also proactive foresight.

Firstly, it's crucial to recognize that digital backlashes are a natural byproduct of today's democratized communication channels. The immediacy of these platforms means anyone with internet access can voice their dissent, potentially causing a tidal wave of negative publicity. Whether stemming from a genuine grievance or a misunderstanding, the virality of such incidents can catch even the most prepared leader off guard. Awareness and preparedness are your first lines of defense, allowing you to anticipate potential flashpoints before they ignite.

At the heart of effectively responding to digital backlash lies a comprehensive understanding of your audience and their expectations. This goes beyond mere demographics and delves into the emotive aspects of public sentiment. When a crisis emerges, it's important to step back and analyze not just the facts but the feelings. What are people truly upset about? Sometimes, a backlash reflects deeper concerns about trust or transparency that have been simmering beneath the surface.

Crafting an appropriate response requires a blend of authenticity and strategic thinking. A hasty reply, intended to douse the flames, may inadvertently add fuel to the fire if perceived as insincere or dismissive. Instead, leaders should take time to formulate responses that acknowledge the core issues at hand while aligning with their broader values and mission. Remember, in the digital age, transparency isn't just a policy—it's a survival tactic.

Consider the use of digital tools analytics here as an ally rather than an afterthought. Monitoring platforms can offer real-time insights into how the backlash is evolving and who the key influencers are. With this data, leaders can tailor their responses to address not only the most vocal critics but also the silent majority who might be swayed by convincing dialogue. It's a dance of diplomacy where every step—every tweet, post, or comment—should be measured and intentional.

Engagement is another crucial component of handling digital backlashes. People want to feel heard, understood, and respected. This means actively engaging with your audience, addressing their concerns directly, and fostering genuine dialogue. While an official statement might clarify the company's position, oftentimes it's the personal interactions—a responding tweet, a video message from the leader—that humanize the situation and mend bridges.

Moreover, timing is everything. Swift response is vital, yet it's equally important to communicate when you've fully grasped the dimensions of the issue. An initial acknowledgment followed by a more detailed plan can be a solid approach. Adrian Bosch, a leader known for his adept handling of public relations, once noted, "In the digital age, speed combined with empathy wins the race." While his context was different, the principle transcends scenarios.

As historical contexts teach us, when under siege, avoid retreat. Instead, fortify your position, learn from the criticism, and adapt accordingly. Sometimes, a digital backlash might highlight weaknesses in your strategy, policy, or product—view these insights as opportunities for growth. It's in these moments that resilient leaders foster innovation and create value from adversity.

In a digital age saturated with opinions, the art of gracefully handling criticism can transform potential setbacks into leaps of progress. Returning to our Machiavellian roots, remember that maintaining power involves both strategic intellect and a subtle touch of dexterity. When adeptly managed, backlashes can be turned into platforms for demonstrating commitment to listening, learning, and improving.

Ultimately, digital backlashes are not enemies to be vanquished. They represent a dialogue—a tumultuous one, perhaps—that challenges leaders to rethink, reimagine, and recalibrate. As long as the leader remains steady, informed, and compassionate, they'll find their footing even in the stormiest of digital seas.

As we close this section, the emphasis remains on wisdom garnered through experience and the foresight of anticipatory strategizing. It's about learning from digital echoes, adjusting the sails, and steering the narrative toward resolution and reaffirmation of mission and integrity. When the sand of controversy settles, the mark of a great leader is not just surviving a digital backlash, but thriving in its wake.

## Strategies for Digital Resilience

As the modern leader navigates the tumultuous waters of the digital world, mastering digital resilience is not just an asset but a necessity. In a hyperconnected environment where information travels at the speed of light and opinions shift with the fleeting winds of social media, knowing how to stand firm amidst chaos is paramount. Resilience in the digital age goes beyond simply bouncing back; it encompasses the foresight to anticipate challenges, the agility to adapt, and the wisdom to transform setbacks into stepping stones.

The first element of digital resilience involves having a proactive stance. It's essential for leaders to recognize potential digital pitfalls before they materialize. This prescience comes from a deep understanding of digital trends and an organization's vulnerabilities. Regular risk assessments and threat modeling are not just tools for IT departments—they are strategic imperatives for leadership.

Consider the importance of building a robust digital infrastructure. A strong, secure foundation facilitates agility and shields the organization from some digital disruptions. Invest in cutting-edge security protocols, constant updates, and comprehensive backup systems. An organization's resilience is only as strong as its weakest link; hence, leadership should ensure stringent cybersecurity practices permeate every level of the organization.

Communication, as always, remains a linchpin in crisis management. During tumultuous times, transparent and consistent communication reassures stakeholders. Leaders must embrace digital communication channels to maintain a coherent narrative amidst chaos. This means not only addressing external audiences but also ensuring internal communications are clear and supportive, providing teams with the guidance they need to navigate crises effectively.

Beyond infrastructure and communication, cultivating a resilient organizational culture is key. Foster an environment where adaptability and innovation are celebrated. Encourage teams to experiment, learn from failures, and iterate on their successes. When people know they can rely on a culture that supports measured risk-taking and innovation, they approach crises with optimism and creativity.

Acknowledging the inevitability of digital crises, leaders should develop comprehensive response plans. These plans should be dynamic, allowing room for adaptation as the situation evolves. Test these plans regularly through simulations and drills to ensure preparedness. Involving a cross-functional team in these exercises ensures broader perspectives and expertise in crisis management.

Monitoring and response mechanisms should be attuned to digital signals. Social listening tools and analytics offer a window into the public's perception, revealing emerging issues before they escalate. Equipping teams with these tools allows for timely interventions, mitigating potential damage.

After managing a digital crisis, reflection and learning become pivotal. A resilient leader understands that each crisis is a lesson laden with insights. Conduct thorough post-mortems to evaluate what unfolded, what worked, and what didn't. This feedback loop is crucial for refining strategies and strengthening future responses.

Moreover, nurturing partnerships and collaborations can enhance an organization's resilience. Establish alliances with other players in the industry who can offer support and share insights during a crisis. A network of allies can provide resources, advice, and a united front when needed.

No matter how well-prepared, crises will test even the most resilient leader. Emotional resilience is equally crucial. Leaders should develop the mental fortitude to remain calm and decisive under pressure. Prioritizing mental health and well-being, both for oneself and one's team, lays the groundwork for handling crises with grace.

In conclusion, digital resilience isn't just about withstanding the storm; it's about emerging stronger and wiser. By embedding resilience into the very fabric of their organizations, leaders craft not only a robust defense against digital upheavals but also a foundation for sustainable success. In an age where change is constant, resilience is the bedrock upon which modern leadership is built.

# Chapter 9:
# Innovation and Adaptability

In the ever-evolving landscape of the digital age, innovation and adaptability have emerged as indispensable traits for contemporary leaders determined to redefine paradigms and mold the future. As the pace of technological change accelerates, those who embrace creative thinking and welcome new ideas become the architects of their own destiny, navigating uncharted territories with confidence and foresight. Successful leaders cultivate an environment where experimentation thrives and failure is not a setback but a stepping stone toward profound discoveries. This mindset not only fuels organizational growth but also inspires teams to push boundaries and rally behind a shared vision of progress. By integrating transformative technologies with strategic adaptability, leaders can harness the unpredictable currents of change, propelling themselves and their organizations toward previously unimaginable heights of achievement and influence.

## Encouraging Creative Thinking

In today's fast-paced, tech-driven world, fostering creativity isn't just about generating new ideas—it's about cultivating a mindset that's open to innovation and adaptability. The digital landscape demands leaders who not only welcome change but also thrive on it. To master this art, one must carefully blend Machiavellian strategies with modern digital ingenuity, encouraging a culture where creative thinking isn't the exception but the rule.

Creativity can often seem elusive, particularly within environments defined by constant change and pressure. Yet, it's precisely in these spaces that fresh ideas and innovative solutions can flourish if the right conditions are established. Essentially, creativity must be seen as a critical element of strategic leadership rather than an optional exercise in brainstorming. Leaders who see creativity as indispensable to digital strategy can navigate complexities with greater ease and effectiveness.

As modern leaders adapt Machiavelli's lessons, the challenge lies in harnessing the power of creative thinking to steer both themselves and their teams towards impactful outcomes. Encouraging creativity starts with building a safe space for ideas to be freely expressed and explored. This doesn't mean leaving strategy to chance, but rather integrating creative processes into every facet of decision-making. It's about channeling unorthodox thinking into productive business practices.

Establishing a culture of innovation requires leaders to be role models in practicing creativity. By openly embracing new ideas and showing a willingness to take calculated risks, leaders set a precedent for their teams. This approach dismantles barriers that usually stifle innovation—such as fear of failure or excessive rigidity. Leaders must underscore the importance of learning from failures rather than letting them inhibit progress. After all, many of history's greatest breakthroughs were born from obstacles and failures that sparked new insights.

Ensuring a team feels empowered to innovate means removing the traditional constraints of hierarchy. In this digital age, where hierarchies are flattened and teams are often decentralized, leaders should inspire by connecting ideas across different disciplines and encouraging interdisciplinary collaboration. Such connections often lead to groundbreaking ideas, as insights gained in disparate fields can offer fresh perspectives on familiar challenges.

Technology, too, plays a pivotal role in fostering creative thinking. The vast amounts of data available today provide unprecedented opportunities for innovation. But data in itself is not enough; the key is to convert information into insight. By leveraging technologies such as artificial intelligence and machine learning, digital leaders can make informed decisions that open new pathways for creative solutions.

Yet, the allure of technology can sometimes lead to a paradox: over-reliance on digital tools might stifle creativity rather than enhance it. Therefore, leaders should aim for a balance, utilizing technology as a conduit for creativity, not a replacement for human ingenuity. Encouraging regular digital detoxes and moments of unplugged reflection can help teams reconnect with their imaginative capacities.

An essential aspect of encouraging creative thinking is fostering an environment that celebrates diversity. Diversity of thought, experience, and background enriches the creative process and leads to more robust innovations. By assembling teams with varied perspectives, leaders can tap into a wider range of ideas and solutions, which is crucial for staying relevant and competitive in a global digital economy.

Moreover, creativity thrives in environments that continuously engage the curiosity of the team. Leaders can ignite this curiosity by promoting a culture of ongoing learning and exploration. Encouraging team members to pursue new interests, attend seminars, and engage with emerging technologies can lead to unexpected inspirations. Leaders should also encourage reflection and dialogue about how new learnings could apply to current strategies.

Modern leaders must also recognize the creative potential that resides in chaos and ambiguity. Rather than seeking to quell disruption, they should harness it as a chance to pivot and innovate. The ability to remain agile in the face of change and to pivot resources towards new opportunities often distinguishes successful leaders from the rest.

Ultimately, encouraging creative thinking in a digital world isn't just about generating ideas—it's about cultivating a culture that values and systematically integrates them. Modern leaders must envision creativity not as a sporadic brilliance but as a sustained strategic asset. By embedding creative thinking into the core values of their leadership approach, they can navigate the evolving complexities of the digital age and lead with vision, acumen, and boldness that defines true digital trailblazers.

Integrating these principles in leadership requires intentionality, flexibility, and an ever-evolving approach to learning and growth. By encouraging creativity at every level, leaders not only drive innovation but also ensure their organizations are poised to thrive in an unpredictable future. This creates a dynamic environment where both people and processes evolve in synergy, fostering a leadership legacy that reflects both the wisdom of Machiavelli and the possibilities of the digital age.

## Embracing Technological Change

As we continue our exploration into the realm of innovation and adaptability, the concept of embracing technological change naturally surfaces as both a challenge and an opportunity for modern leaders. Change, especially when driven by technology, can be as daunting as it is exhilarating. For those who shy away from the unknown, the rapid pace of technological evolution can seem like a formidable adversary. Yet, for those willing to embrace it, technology offers an unprecedented avenue to redefine what leadership looks like in our interconnected world.

Innovation doesn't merely knock at the door; it often barges in unannounced, disrupting the tranquility of familiar routines. The transformational potential inherent in technological advancements is immense. We're talking about tools that can optimize operations, platforms that can amplify a leader's voice, and networks that can extend one's influence around the globe. But with great power comes the responsibility to wield it wisely. Embracing change requires a careful balance between maintaining the core values that define effective leadership and being open to the shifts that new technologies mandate.

Consider the rise of artificial intelligence and machine learning, which are not just buzzwords but actual game changers in decision-making processes. Leaders today have access to more data and insights than ever before, allowing them to make informed decisions swiftly. However, the key lies not in merely accumulating data but in discerning how to use it effectively. This ability to interpret and integrate technology into strategic planning is what distinguishes the leaders of tomorrow from those anchored in the past.

Innovation is often born out of necessity—a response to challenges that seem insurmountable without fresh thinking. In many ways, the digital revolution has become a crucible for testing the mettle of leaders. Those who thrive do so not by clinging to the vestiges of past success but by viewing every technological leap as a stepping stone to future possibilities. The adaptability mindset is about viewing change not as a loss of control but as an expansion of the potential for growth.

Technological change is also reshaping the traditional structures of power. Hierarchies are being flattened, and networks are taking precedence over top-down commands. Leaders now find themselves negotiating these new terrains where influence often stems from networked collaborations rather than positional authority. This democratization of influence allows agile leaders to foster environments where ideas flow freely and innovation flourishes. It's in these vibrant spaces that leaders can most effectively steer their organizations and initiatives towards success.

Moreover, the advent of technology in leadership requires a cultural shift within organizations. It's not enough for a leader to adopt new tools; they must cultivate a culture that accepts and even anticipates change. This involves inspiring teams to embrace lifelong learning, encouraging experimentation, and most importantly, allowing space for failure within the innovation process. Transformative leaders understand that failure is not the opposite of success but a crucial part of the journey towards it.

It's important to remember that at the heart of technological change is a simpler truth: a desire to enhance the human experience. The digital tools we leverage should serve to augment our capabilities and bridge distances between us. Whether it's through virtual reality, which brings far-flung teams together, or through sophisticated communication platforms that boost collaboration, tech-driven change is ultimately about enhancing human connections and capabilities.

While some may argue that technology threatens to dehumanize leadership, the true challenge—and skill—is ensuring that it does the opposite. It's about using technology to amplify human traits such as empathy, creativity, and vision. When properly integrated, technological changes can lead to more personalized interactions and deeper understanding among colleagues and clients alike.

The leaders who stand out in the digital age are those who keep one eye on the horizon while remaining grounded in the realities of now. Their vision is futuristic but their actions are firmly rooted in the present. Embracing technological change is a dynamic process; it involves continuous learning, adapting, and applying what's learned to create meaningful progress.

In conclusion, embracing technological change is less about technological mastery and more about fostering an adaptive, innovative mindset. It's about using technology as a conduit for possibility rather than a deterrent to tradition. Modern leaders must become comfortable with being uncomfortable, for it's on this edge of uncertainty that the greatest innovations are born.

# Chapter 10:
# Building and Leading
# Virtual Teams

In today's digital landscape, building and leading virtual teams has evolved from a novel challenge into a vital skill for modern leaders. The art of virtual team leadership draws parallels to Machiavellian tactics, demanding keen strategy and adaptability. In hyperconnected environments, fostering collaboration online transcends mere convenience; it becomes an essential driver of success. Leaders who master this can blend technological prowess with profound human insight, creating environments that inspire trust and innovation. To maintain team engagement across digital divides, one must be adept at leveraging diverse communication tools while cultivating a culture of transparency and inclusivity. Visionaries in this space recognize the nuances of digital body language and actively harness them to bridge gaps, crafting a cohesive narrative that binds individuals into a formidable, unified cohort. As we delve deeper into the nuances of digital leadership, it becomes evident that those who can guide dispersed teams with clarity and empathy will stand as the architects of the future, transforming virtual crossroads into pathways of unprecedented potential.

## Fostering Collaboration Online

In today's fast-paced digital world, fostering collaboration online isn't just a cornerstone of effective leadership—it's a necessity. As teams spread across continents and time zones, the traditional dynamics of teamwork have evolved into a vibrant, interconnected web of digital touchpoints. To navigate this landscape successfully, leaders must harness the power of virtual collaboration tools and embrace new strategies to engage and empower their teams.

At the heart of online collaboration lies communication. Clear and transparent communication is the backbone of any collaborative effort, and in a virtual setting, it becomes even more critical. Leaders need to employ a mix of synchronous and asynchronous communication tools to ensure that everyone stays in the loop. While video conferences can simulate face-to-face interactions and build rapport, asynchronous platforms like collaborative documents and messaging apps ensure that ideas flow constantly, not just during scheduled meetings.

Digital tools are just one part of the equation. The human element—trust, empathy, and shared purpose—plays an equally significant role in fostering collaboration. Leaders must work diligently to create a culture where team members feel safe to share their ideas and opinions, knowing they are valued and respected. This sense of psychological safety encourages innovation and ensures that diverse perspectives are integrated into problem-solving processes.

Furthermore, it's important to recognize the differences in communication styles and cultural backgrounds within a virtual team. What might be a direct and straightforward message for one person could be perceived as blunt or even rude by another. Here, emotional intelligence becomes a key competency for leaders. By tuning into the nuances of digital body language and being considerate of diverse viewpoints, leaders can mediate potential conflicts and build bridges between team members.

The very tools that facilitate connection can also become points of friction if not used wisely. Leaders need to be strategic in their choice and implementation of technology, selecting platforms and tools that align with the team's needs and workflows. This intentional approach helps to prevent tool fatigue and ensures that technology enhances rather than hinders collaboration.

Establishing clear norms and expectations around virtual interactions is also essential. Norms provide a roadmap for team behavior, guiding how team members participate in meetings, share tasks, or provide feedback. By defining these boundaries early on, leaders can streamline interactions, reduce misunderstandings, and foster a cohesive team environment, even across digital divides.

One practical strategy for enhancing online collaboration is setting up regular check-ins. These interactions provide structured opportunities for team members to align objectives, celebrate successes, and address any roadblocks. Check-ins can vary in frequency and format depending on the team's needs, but their consistent presence can reinforce a team's commitment to shared goals and improve overall accountability.

Leaders should also leverage the power of shared digital spaces—not just for work-related tasks, but for building camaraderie. Virtual coffee breaks, online game sessions, or casual chat channels can serve as digital water coolers, enabling team members to connect on a personal level. This humanization of the virtual experience helps strengthen the social fabric of the team, which can affect how effectively they collaborate on projects.

Moreover, recognizing and celebrating individual and group achievements is crucial in an online environment. Meritocracy, when practiced correctly, goes a long way in motivating team members and recognizing their contributions. Public acknowledgments using digital badges or shout-outs during meetings can boost morale and encourage a culture of excellence.

Alongside recognition, leaders must become adept at giving and receiving feedback online. Effective feedback is timely, specific, and constructive, and digital channels provide unique opportunities to document and revisit these conversations as needed. Regular feedback dialogues help create a growth-oriented atmosphere where team members are encouraged to develop their skills continuously.

Finally, leaders must remain adaptable, continuously refining their online collaboration strategies based on feedback and evolving team dynamics. By actively seeking input from their teams, leaders can ensure that collaboration methods remain effective and relevant, adapting to changing needs and circumstances.

In essence, fostering collaboration online isn't simply about selecting the right digital tools—it's about creating an environment where innovation thrives and all team members feel connected and valued. By cultivating a culture of trust, transparency, and mutual respect, modern leaders can effectively steer their virtual teams through the complexities of the digital age, transforming potential challenges into opportunities for growth and success.

## Maintaining Team Engagement

In the quest to lead virtual teams effectively, maintaining engagement is akin to the lifeblood that keeps the digital machine running smoothly. Engaged team members are more productive, innovative, and committed. It's no longer just about assembling a team; it's about nurturing a vibrant community that thrives even when members are scattered across different time zones and cultural backgrounds.

Treating team engagement as a top priority can give you a strategic edge. It's crucial for leaders to recognize that engagement isn't static; it's a dynamic state that requires continual attention and nurturing. While traditional leadership relied on physical presence to gauge sentiment and productivity, the virtual environment demands a different approach, one that leverages technology and psychological insights to keep the team motivated and connected.

Start with clear communication. In a virtual setting, clarity becomes paramount. Miscommunication or lack of information can easily lead to disengagement. Leaders should establish regular check-ins, using these opportunities to provide feedback, share goals, and encourage team members. But it's not just about frequency; it's also about creating an open dialogue where team members feel valued and heard. This can be facilitated by using various digital tools that enable seamless communication, whether through video, chat, or collaborative platforms.

Building a culture of trust and accountability is another cornerstone of maintaining engagement. In the absence of face-to-face interactions, trust is built through consistency, transparency, and reliability in communication. Encourage team members to take ownership of their tasks and celebrate their successes publicly. This public acknowledgment goes a long way in boosting morale and reinforcing positive behaviors.

Personal connections shouldn't be underestimated. While virtual teams may miss the impromptu water-cooler conversations, leaders can create virtual spaces that mimic these informal interactions. Consider initiating casual video meetings that encourage team members to share personal achievements or discuss topics outside work. These interactions can fortify bonds, making cooperation more fluid and spontaneous.

Additionally, it's essential to foster an environment that encourages creativity and adaptability. This involves advocating for a workplace culture that rewards innovative thinking and doesn't penalize failure. A stimulated team is far more likely to be an engaged one. Giving team members the freedom to experiment and contribute ideas without fear of retribution encourages active participation and loyalty.

Feedback loops also play a critical role in maintaining engagement. Regularly solicit feedback from team members to understand their needs and frustrations. This insight is invaluable for making necessary adjustments and showing the team that their input matters, further fostering an engaged, collaborative environment.

Consider equipping your team with the right technology. Digital tools that promote collaboration and connectivity can significantly enhance engagement by making everyone's work easier and faster. When team members have the tools they need to do their job effectively, they are more likely to remain engaged and invested in their work.

Besides technology, consider the psychological aspect of leadership. Empathy and emotional intelligence are significant facets of leading virtual teams. They are crucial in understanding team members' challenges and providing support that addresses their specific circumstances. Remember, engagement is as much about heart as it is about mind.

Lastly, tailor your approach to engagement according to your team's unique makeup. Each team is a microcosm with its individual dynamics and cultures. What works for one group may not resonate with another. As a leader, keen observation, flexibility, and a deep understanding of your team are your greatest allies in crafting a strategy that keeps everyone engaged and thriving.

Nurturing a highly engaged virtual team isn't just an operational choice; it's a strategic imperative. By fostering an engaging, connected, and empowered team culture, you're not only enhancing productivity but also building a resilient framework that can weather the challenges of a constantly evolving digital landscape.

# Chapter 11:
# Harnessing Digital Tools
# for Leadership

In today's rapidly evolving tech landscape, the arsenal of digital tools available to leaders isn't just a luxury; it's a necessity for navigating the complex web of modern leadership. These tools empower leaders to streamline operations, enhance productivity, and stay ahead in competitive markets. From project management software that allows a real-time overview of team progress to analytics platforms that offer insights into consumer behavior, digital tools provide essential capabilities for decision-making and strategic foresight. Embracing these technologies can transform an organization's ability to pivot swiftly in response to market demands, empowering leaders to make informed decisions with greater speed and precision. However, the true prowess of a digital leader is marked not just by mastering these tools but by harnessing them to cultivate a culture of innovation and adaptability. By leveraging technology effectively, modern leaders can create environments where creativity flourishes and where the digital enables rather than encumbers, leading to tangible and sustained success.

## Essential Tech for Modern Leaders

Today's world is a labyrinth of digital tools, and for modern leaders, navigating this complex environment is not just an option; it's a necessity. As leaders strive to stay ahead, the key lies in understanding which technologies are essential to drive success. The fusion of strategic thinking with the right tech arsenal transforms leaders from being merely competent to truly visionary.

First and foremost, cloud technology has revolutionized the way leaders manage resources. It's no longer about what hardware sits in your office; it's about accessing the massive computing power offered by services like AWS and Azure. These cloud platforms provide unprecedented flexibility and scalability, allowing leaders to deploy applications, store vast amounts of data, and scale operations with ease. Emphasizing agility, they enable leaders to respond swiftly to the demands of the market without the burden of managing physical infrastructure.

Then there's data analytics—an essential tool for informed decision-making. Data-driven insights can be a game-changer in crafting strategies and understanding market dynamics. By utilizing advanced analytics tools such as Power BI or Tableau, leaders can transform raw data into powerful insights, revealing patterns that were previously hidden. The ability to visualize data in meaningful ways fosters better communication of ideas and facilitates strategic forecasting.

Collaboration tools ensure that teams remain connected, no matter where they are in the world. Platforms like Slack and Microsoft Teams have become indispensable in fostering communication across virtual teams. These tools embed seamless integration with various services, allowing for document sharing, video conferencing, and instant messaging, all within one application. The result? Faster decision-making and a more cohesive team structure.

Security is another aspect that cannot be ignored. As cyber threats become more sophisticated, leaders must adopt cutting-edge security technologies to safeguard their digital assets. Implementing multi-factor authentication, robust encryption protocols, and endpoint security solutions are all integral to building a fortified digital environment. It's about being proactive rather than reactive, ensuring that data breaches and cyber attacks are swiftly mitigated.

Project management tools are transforming the efficacy with which leaders oversee and execute operations. Software like Monday.com and Asana allows leaders to outline tasks, set deadlines, and track progress with real-time updates. These tools provide transparency within teams and across organizational departments, making it easier to ensure that everyone is aligned with the overarching goals.

Moreover, customer relationship management (CRM) systems such as Salesforce are quintessential in managing interactions with customers. They offer a holistic view of customer engagement, enabling personalized communication that leads to higher satisfaction and retention rates. By tapping into CRM systems, leaders can create more meaningful interactions, building a loyal customer base that propels the organization forward.

In the realm of marketing, social media management tools like Hootsuite have unlocked new potentials for leaders. These platforms allow leaders to manage their brand's voice across multiple channels efficiently. Whether it's scheduling posts or analyzing engagement metrics, these tools aid leaders in amplifying their brand presence and staying relevant in ever-changing social landscapes.

For leaders looking to leverage AI, platforms that offer machine learning capabilities unlock opportunities to enhance operations. AI tools can automate repetitive tasks, freeing up human capital for more strategic initiatives. Additionally, AI can drive personalization at scale, providing deeper customer insights, which leads to more impactful marketing campaigns and improved customer experiences.

Video conferencing tools like Zoom have become non-negotiables in an era where in-person meetings are less frequent. These technologies allow leaders to maintain face-to-face interaction, which is crucial for building relationships and nurturing trust within teams. High-quality video communication breaks down geographic barriers, making collaboration more dynamic and inclusive.

As leaders, embracing these technologies involves not just understanding their functions but integrating them into the fabric of the organization. The challenge lies in weaving these tools into everyday operations in a way that augments rather than disrupts. By doing so, leaders set the stage for enhanced productivity, innovation, and competitiveness.

In conclusion, essential tech tools provide leaders with more than just operational efficiency; they are the levers of strategic advantage. With each digital tool adopted, leaders are better equipped to navigate the complexities of the modern business landscape. The journey to mastery involves not only embracing these technologies but also continuously reevaluating and adapting them to align with the organization's mission and goals. By doing so, modern leaders transform into catalysts, leading their teams and organizations to thrive in an ever-evolving digital world.

## Streamlining Operations with Technology

Embracing technology to streamline operations is not just a strategy—it's a necessity in today's fast-paced, digital-first world. What was once considered efficient a few years back has now evolved, and leaders are called upon to rethink their processes profoundly. This transformation is akin to a modern-day Renaissance, where innovation leads the way much like it did in times of old, but the tools and techniques have changed significantly. For modern leaders, harnessing digital tools effectively is paramount to remaining relevant and competitive.

The first step in streamlining operations with technology is recognizing the specific needs of your organization. Every business is different; what works for one company might not be appropriate for another. Leaders must conduct a detailed assessment of their existing workflows and identify areas ripe for technological intervention. This doesn't mean replacing the human touch with machines entirely but rather finding a harmonious balance that enhances human capabilities.

In streamlining operations, automation plays a pivotal role. By automating routine processes, leaders can free up valuable human resources to focus on more strategic, creative tasks. Think about customer service bots that handle inquiries round the clock, or finance software that automatically categorizes and manages expenses. Automation can greatly increase efficiency, reduce errors, and allow teams to focus on strategic initiatives rather than getting bogged down with routine administrative tasks.

However, while automation offers substantial benefits, it must be implemented thoughtfully. It's crucial to ensure that the human touch, which is integral to customer satisfaction and employee engagement, isn't lost in the quest for efficiency. The challenge is in finding the right blend—using technology to enhance human effort without overshadowing it. Instead of seeing technology and humanity as opposing forces, leaders should view them as complementary.

Beyond automation, data analytics provides another powerful tool for streamlining operations. Leaders can use vast amounts of data to gain insights, predict trends, and make informed decisions quickly. Data-driven leadership means having the right information at your fingertips when you need it. Whether it's understanding customer behavior, forecasting sales, or optimizing supply chains, data can be the light that guides decision-makers through the maze of modern business challenges.

Data's powerful role in streamlining operations cannot be overstated. However, it's not just about collecting and analyzing data; it's about translating those insights into actionable strategies that improve business processes. Leaders need to cultivate a culture where data isn't just gathered but is actively used to drive measurable improvements. This means investing in the right tools and technologies that can turn raw data into clear insights, and training teams to interpret and act on this information.

No conversation about streamlining operations with technology would be complete without mentioning collaboration tools. In today's interconnected world, teams are often spread out globally, requiring robust digital solutions to bridge the physical divide. Tools like project management software, communication platforms, and cloud-based document sharing enable seamless collaboration, ensuring that distance doesn't become a barrier to productivity and innovation.

Modern leaders must champion a shift towards a digital-first mindset, where technology facilitates not just communication, but collaboration at all levels of the organization. By doing so, they can foster environments that are more agile, responsive, and creative. It is about creating a workplace where ideas can flow freely, and collaboration becomes the norm rather than the exception.

However, transitioning to digital operations isn't without its challenges. Security remains a top concern, especially with the increasing frequency and sophistication of cyber threats. As leaders streamline operations through technology, they must also develop robust cybersecurity practices to protect sensitive information and maintain trust with stakeholders. It's about balancing openness and security—making sure that your systems are both accessible and protected.

As technology continues to evolve at an unprecedented pace, leaders must remain both adaptable and forward-thinking. Streamlining operations with today's technology sets the stage for harnessing the tools of tomorrow. Leaders should stay informed about emerging technologies that could further enhance operational efficiency. This requires a commitment to lifelong learning and an openness to change and innovation.

In conclusion, streamlining operations with technology isn't a one-time project—it's an ongoing journey. Leaders who embrace this journey will find themselves at the forefront of their industries, able to navigate the complexities of the modern digital landscape with agility and precision. By leveraging technology thoughtfully, leaders can reimagine operations and, in doing so, redefine what is possible for their organizations.

# Chapter 12:
# Leading Through Change
# and Disruption

In a world where technology evolves faster than ever, leading through change and disruption requires more than just adaptation—it demands a visionary approach. Modern leaders must embrace the relentless pace of change, crafting strategies that not only address immediate challenges but also prepare organizations for the unknown. This involves fostering a culture where adaptability isn't just encouraged, it's ingrained in the organizational DNA. Leaders should guide their teams through the ebb and flow of innovation by nurturing an environment that prizes curiosity, resilience, and proactive problem-solving. As disruption becomes a constant companion, it transforms from a threat into an opportunity for growth, allowing leaders to reimagine their role and redefine the possible. In doing so, they don't just react to the firestorms of change but instead become adept navigators of the digital tempest, steering their organizations toward a future marked by agility and sustained success. In this context, change is less a hurdle and more a catalyst for unlocking untapped potential within the workforce and broader market landscape.

## Navigating Constant Evolution

In a world where change is the only constant, leaders face the daunting task of steering their organizations through uncharted waters. The rapid pace of technological advancement and the shifting sands of the digital landscape present unique challenges. Today's leaders must be visionaries—quick to anticipate trends and agile enough to adapt to them. How can one remain steadfast in a world that refuses to stand still? It requires a precise balance of foresight, adaptability, and resilience. There is no room for complacency when the future is being rewritten every day.

The art of leadership in dynamic environments rests heavily on understanding and embracing change. Just as Machiavelli perceived the need to navigate the complexities of power in his era, modern leaders must master the intricacies of a continually evolving digital world. This requires not just a strategy but a mindset—an acceptance that evolution is not merely a phenomena; it's an opportunity. Leaders today need to learn how to harness the winds of change rather than be buffeted by them.

As we analyze the contours of constant evolution, it becomes clear that adaptability is not just a trait—it's a necessity. In practical terms, this means becoming comfortable with uncertainty and risk. Leaders need to be flexible enough to pivot their strategies when the circumstances demand it. However, this flexibility must be informed by solid data and guided by a well-defined vision. The best leaders are those who can transform ambiguity into opportunity, using limited information to make decisions that drive their organizations forward.

One vital aspect of navigating constant evolution is the ability to foresee change before it happens. This doesn't imply possessing a crystal ball but developing the foresight to recognize patterns and signals in the present that indicate future shifts. This predictive capability can be cultivated through rigorous analysis of current trends, engaging with forward-thinking thinkers, and constant learning. Leaders who immerse themselves in diverse knowledge pools increase their chances of spotting the next big disruption before it arrives on their doorstep.

Furthermore, evolution in a digital context calls for leaders to foster an innovative culture within their organizations. Encouraging teams to think outside the box, experiment with new ideas, and learn from failures can unlock a treasure trove of potential. This involves building an environment where creative thinking thrives, and team members are not shackled by the fear of failure. The most successful organizations of the digital age are those that view each failed experiment as a stepping stone towards a groundbreaking discovery.

While adaptability is crucial, it shouldn't come at the expense of stability. Leaders must ensure that their core values remain intact, acting as a guiding light as they navigate change. A clearly defined mission and set of values can provide a rudder of stability amidst the chaos that evolution can sometimes bring. It's crucial to communicate these values clearly throughout the organization, so every team member understands the direction toward which the company strives.

It is equally important to build a resilient workforce. The turbulence of constant evolution can take its toll on employee morale and productivity. Thus, leaders should invest in creating a supportive work environment where employees feel empowered to tackle challenges head-on. Providing ongoing learning opportunities and emphasizing mental well-being can create an atmosphere where resilience is cultivated naturally.

The digital age also presents leaders with an unprecedented ability to tap into global perspectives. Integration of diverse insights can enrich decision-making processes, enabling leaders to view change through a multifaceted lens. By creating networks that transcend geographical boundaries, leaders can better anticipate global shifts that might affect their local operations.

As much as we discuss the future, the present cannot be neglected. Continual evaluation of current processes and initiatives ensures that organizations remain poised for what's next. This can involve harnessing analytics to evaluate performance, KPIs to track progress, and agile project management frameworks to iterate efficiently. Effective leaders always have their finger on the pulse of their enterprise, ready to adjust tactics when evidence suggests a change in course.

In sum, navigating constant evolution calls for a holistic approach—one that blends strategic foresight with agile execution. It's about finding harmony between adaptation and tradition, innovation and stability. Leaders who master this balance will not only survive the digital revolution but thrive within it, poised to meet the challenges and seize the opportunities of tomorrow.

Change is daunting, and the path forward is not always clear. Yet, Machiavelli's wisdom endures, urging us not to shy away from uncertainty but to embrace it. By doing so, leaders can transform potential disruptions into their greatest triumphs, heralding an era where change isn't feared but celebrated. In the end, the leaders who excel are those who see evolution not merely as a challenge, but as a canvas for pioneering, leading their organizations into new frontiers with courage and confidence.

## Building a Culture of Adaptability

In today's ever-evolving digital landscape, adaptability isn't just a beneficial trait—it's a fundamental necessity. The ability to swiftly adjust to new circumstances is what sets successful leaders apart from the rest. However, creating a culture of adaptability requires deliberate strategy and clear vision, especially amidst continuous change and disruption. It's not just about reacting to the latest trends or technologies but about embedding the capacity to foresee changes and pivot proactively.

Adaptability begins with leadership that embraces change rather than resists it. Leaders must model flexibility and openness, encouraging their teams to perceive change as an opportunity rather than a threat. This shift in mindset can transform hesitation into eagerness, fostering an environment where innovation thrives. Leaders who are adaptable often demonstrate a unique blend of confidence and humility, acknowledging that while they may not have all the answers, they're always ready to explore new paths.

To build a culture of adaptability, it's crucial to maintain a diverse and inclusive team. Diversity brings a wealth of perspectives, facilitating creative problem-solving and innovation. A team comprising individuals from varied backgrounds can analyze challenges from multiple angles, making it easier to identify opportunities for improvement and adaptation. In fostering diversity, leaders also promote a culture of continuous learning, where every voice contributes to the collective intelligence of the group.

Encouraging risk-taking without the fear of failure is another cornerstone of adaptability. In a culture where innovation is paramount, mistakes should be seen as stepping stones to success. Leaders can cultivate this atmosphere by recognizing and rewarding calculated risks and celebrating both successes and failures as learning opportunities. Open debriefs after failed initiatives can offer invaluable insights, refining future strategies and reinforcing a resilient organizational mindset.

An adaptable culture also hinges on effective communication. Transparent communication channels keep everyone informed and engaged, reducing uncertainty and speculation during times of change. Leaders should prioritize open dialogues, ensuring that all team members have a clear understanding of changes, their implications, and the role of each individual in the transition process. Regular updates and feedback loops help maintain alignment with organizational goals while fostering trust and collaboration.

Moreover, leveraging technology can exponentially increase a team's adaptability. Digital tools for collaboration, data analysis, and communication can streamline transitions and provide real-time insights into shifting landscapes. It's essential for leaders to stay abreast of emerging technologies and consider how they might be integrated into their business models to enhance flexibility. The strategic use of such technologies can turn potential disruptions into opportunities for growth.

Embracing adaptability also requires a focus on developing agile processes. Agile methodologies, known for their flexibility and iterative nature, can be powerful in driving adaptability. These methodologies allow teams to work more dynamically, adapting rapidly to change based on frequent feedback and reflection. Implementing agile practices not only enhances productivity but also cultivates a mindset ready for constant evolution.

Training and development play a vital role in fostering adaptability. Equipping team members with the skills needed to navigate and thrive amid change is crucial. Offering continuous learning opportunities, such as workshops or digital courses, can empower employees to update their skills and learn new ways of thinking. Leaders should nurture a growth mindset, encouraging team members to seek knowledge actively and view each change as a learning opportunity.

Furthermore, adaptable organizations often have a strong sense of purpose and alignment with their core values. In times of change, these values act as a compass, guiding decisions and behaviors. When teams are driven by a shared mission, they can maintain clarity and focus, even in turbulent times. Purpose-driven adaptability not only enhances resilience but also strengthens organizational loyalty and employee engagement.

Perhaps the most significant advantage of building a culture of adaptability is its impact on innovation. When adaptability is embedded into a company's DNA, it unlocks the potential for groundbreaking ideas and breakthrough solutions. Organizations that prioritize adaptability are more likely to anticipate trends and react with agility, staying ahead of competitors. They foster a workforce that is not just competent, but also courageous—willing to explore uncharted territories to seize new opportunities.

In conclusion, creating a culture of adaptability is integral to leading through change and disruption. By championing diversity, encouraging risk-taking, leveraging technology, implementing agile processes, and fostering continuous learning, leaders can cultivate a dynamic environment primed for success. An adaptable organization isn't just better equipped to handle change; it's more prepared to lead it, transforming disruption into opportunity and maintaining a competitive edge in the digital age.

# Chapter 13:
# The Role of AI and Automation in Leadership

As the digital landscape rapidly evolves, the infusion of AI and automation into leadership paradigms is not just inevitable but transformative. Modern leaders must master the delicate art of integrating AI strategies while ensuring their own essence remains fundamentally human. This duality requires viewing AI as a tool that amplifies insights, streamlines operations, and potentially frees leaders from mundane tasks, allowing them to focus on higher-order thinking and emotional intelligence. However, with great power comes the responsibility to navigate this space wisely. The challenge lies in maintaining authenticity and empathy as leaders in a tech-driven world where algorithms often speak louder than voices. It's about harnessing data to make informed decisions without losing sight of the human impact, all while ensuring that technology serves as a bridge, not a barrier, to personal connections. By striking this balance, leaders can effectively guide their teams through the currents of change, crafting a future that honors both innovation and humanity.

## Integrating AI Strategies

As we stand on the cusp of a new era of digital leadership, integrating AI strategies into leadership methodologies has become not just advantageous but essential. The relentless pace of technological advancement has reshaped the capabilities and responsibilities of leaders. Today, they must harness AI to not only streamline operations but also inspire innovation and drive strategic growth. But doing so requires foresight, adaptability, and a keen understanding of both AI's potential and limitations.

AI offers unprecedented tools for leaders to analyze complex datasets, predict trends, and make informed decisions with a speed and precision that were previously unimaginable. By integrating AI systems into decision-making processes, leaders can sift through mountains of data to identify patterns and insights that would otherwise remain buried. This empowers them to anticipate market shifts and implement strategies that align with both their organization's goals and the ever-evolving landscape of consumer demands.

However, the integration of AI into leadership is not an endeavor to be undertaken lightly. While AI can augment human capabilities, it's not a substitute for the nuanced judgment and empathy required in leadership. Effective leaders must balance AI-driven insights with the softer, human aspects of decision-making. They must ensure that the use of AI aligns with their organization's values and ethical standards, emphasizing transparency and fairness.

One practical way to begin integrating AI strategies is through the enhancement of customer experiences. AI technologies, such as chatbots and personalized recommendation engines, can significantly improve customer interactions by delivering more personalized and efficient service. Leaders can leverage these tools to build stronger customer relationships, ensuring a seamless fusion of technology and personal touch.

Furthermore, AI's role in talent management cannot be understated. From recruitment to employee engagement, AI-driven analytics can provide leaders with insights into workforce dynamics, helping them to identify skill gaps and anticipate future needs. By understanding these elements, leaders can create targeted development programs that foster a culture of continuous learning and adaptation.

AI also offers game-changing capabilities in operational efficiency and productivity. Automation of routine tasks allows teams to focus on more strategic, creative, and innovative work. Workflow optimization tools, powered by AI, help eliminate bottlenecks and predict potential disruptions, facilitating smoother operations and boosting overall productivity.

The key to successfully integrating AI lies in not treating it as a standalone solution but as a complementary tool within the broader leadership strategy. Leaders should collaborate with technologists, data scientists, and AI experts to tailor AI solutions to the unique needs of their organization. This collaborative approach ensures that AI is leveraged where it can have the most significant impact, enhancing team effectiveness and achieving strategic objectives.

Furthermore, AI holds transformative potential in the realm of innovation. Machine learning algorithms can rapidly analyze research data and test hypotheses, reducing the time it takes to bring new products to market. By fostering an environment that supports AI-driven innovation, leaders can maintain a competitive edge and respond swiftly to emerging opportunities and threats.

To harness the full potential of AI, it's crucial for leaders to cultivate digital literacy within their teams. By fostering an understanding of AI technologies and their applications, leaders can break down resistance and encourage a culture that embraces AI-driven change. This cultural shift is vital, as it empowers teams to continuously identify new avenues for AI integration, fostering a mindset of innovation and progress.

However, successful AI integration requires leaders to remain vigilant about ethical considerations. Issues such as data privacy, algorithmic bias, and the impact on employment must be addressed proactively. Leaders must strive to create AI solutions that are not only effective but also equitable and just, ensuring that the benefits are shared broadly across society.

Ultimately, integrating AI into leadership strategies is about more than just leveraging cutting-edge technologies. It is about redefining leadership for a digital age—where vision, ethics, and humanity are seamlessly intertwined with technological prowess. Leaders who understand and embrace this convergence will be well-equipped to navigate the complexities of a tech-driven world, inspiring their teams and pioneering paths of progress and transformation.

In conclusion, while AI holds vast potential for enhancing leadership capabilities, it is incumbent upon leaders to approach its integration thoughtfully and strategically. By recognizing AI as an enabler of progress rather than a threat, leaders can harness its power to drive innovation, efficiency, and responsible growth. Through this symbiotic relationship with technology, leaders can pave the way for a future where

AI and humanity flourish together, elevating the art of leadership to new heights.

## Staying Human in a Tech-Driven World

As we navigate the ever-evolving landscape of artificial intelligence and automation, a looming question hovers over modern leadership: How do we maintain our humanity in a world increasingly dominated by technology? This balance between being technologically savvy and retaining a human touch is crucial for leaders striving to make a lasting impact. Today, algorithms shape our experiences, decisions are driven by data, and virtual interactions often replace face-to-face communication. Yet, amidst these advancements, the essence of human connection and empathy remains irreplaceable—or so it should.

The first step in staying human is recognizing that technology is a tool, not a replacement for human interaction. Leaders who thrive are those who use AI and automation to enhance their capabilities rather than allowing these tools to dictate their actions. In the words of Machiavelli, adapting to changing conditions is a mark of astute leadership. Today's leader must adapt by understanding when to rely on technology and when human judgment and empathy are paramount.

Empathy, an innate human quality, sometimes seems overshadowed by the precision and efficiency of machines. Yet, it remains the cornerstone of effective leadership. An empathetic leader recognizes the emotions and perspectives of others, creating connections that a machine simply can't replicate. For instance, in navigating team dynamics or managing a crisis, understanding and responding to human emotions is essential. Machines can offer predictions and strategies, but they lack the intuitive grasp of human complexity that an empathetic leader brings to the table.

Communication is another area where remaining human makes a profound difference. While AI can parse vast amounts of data and help craft messages that resonate, leaders must ensure their communications are authentic and sincere. The nuances of tone, body language, and emotional intelligence can't be fully captured by algorithms. Technology can assist but should never overshadow the personal touch and genuine engagement that come from speaking from the heart. In a digital age, authenticity cuts through the noise—it makes leaders relatable and trustworthy.

Yet, being a human-centric leader in a tech-driven world extends beyond empathy and communication. It's about cultivating a sense of purpose and shared values. Employees and stakeholders increasingly seek leaders who stand for something beyond profit and numbers. While AI can enhance productivity, purpose drives passion. A leader who can articulate and embody a clear vision inspires teams to achieve collective goals and foster a shared commitment. This alignment of purpose and vision can't be automated; it's uniquely human.

Of course, staying human also involves embracing vulnerability. Leaders today are expected to be transparent and open about challenges and shortcomings. This openness often leads to deeper trust and stronger relationships with their teams. Machines and algorithms deal in absolutes, but humans grapple with uncertainties and gray areas. Embracing one's imperfections and being honest about them invites collaboration and shared problem-solving. Vulnerability is not a weakness but a powerful catalyst for building deeper connections and inspiring creativity and innovation.

Community, too, plays a vital role in preserving our humanity while leveraging technology. Leaders can learn from communities that seamlessly integrate technology but still prioritize human connections. Whether through online forums, collaborative platforms, or local networks, these spaces provide opportunities for authentic interaction, fostering a sense of belonging and support. As leaders, facilitating and nurturing these communities helps maintain a balance between the digital and the human, ensuring that technology serves as a bridge and not a barrier.

Moreover, ethical considerations take center stage when ensuring that our tech-driven endeavors remain human-focused. In the pursuit of progress and efficiency, leaders must also weigh the impact of their innovations on people and society as a whole. This involves making thoughtful decisions about privacy, data usage, and the implications of automation on jobs and livelihoods. Human-centered leadership calls for a commitment to transparency and integrity, considering not just what technology can do but what it should do.

Finally, staying human in a tech-driven world involves a conscious effort to cultivate creativity and nurture emotional intelligence. As AI handles routine tasks and data analytics, human creativity and strategic thinking become more valuable. Encouraging teams to think outside the box and approach challenges from multiple perspectives fosters an environment where innovation thrives. Emotional intelligence helps leaders navigate the intangible elements of leadership—understanding diverse viewpoints, resolving conflicts, and engendering loyalty and respect.

In conclusion, staying human in a technologically advanced world isn't about rejecting progress but about embracing it with a mindful approach. It requires leaders to engage critically with the tools at their disposal, leaning on them to augment human capabilities while preserving what makes us uniquely human. In doing so, they ensure that the power dynamics of the present and future remain anchored to empathy, authenticity, purpose, and ethical responsibility. As we move forward, the leaders who thrive will be those who've mastered the art of harnessing technology while staying deeply connected to their humanity.

# Chapter 14:
# Networking in a Digital World

In this digital era, the art of networking has transformed beyond face-to-face interactions, demanding a nuanced understanding of virtual landscapes to cultivate influence and power. Today's leaders must harness the vast potential of digital platforms to expand their networks and forge meaningful connections across borders. The essence of digital networking lies in creating authentic relationships that transcend fleeting collaborations, establishing trust and mutual respect in the virtual domain. To navigate this hyperconnected world, one must deftly balance visibility with authenticity, engaging with like-minded individuals while embracing diverse perspectives to drive innovation and adaptability. Whether through social media engagements, virtual conferences, or online forums, the possibilities for connection are as limitless as the ways to leverage these interactions to reinforce one's leadership presence. In mastering the intricacies of digital networking, leaders unlock the doors to unprecedented opportunities for collaboration and influence in the modern age. With every click and connection, the future of leadership unfolds in the hands of those who can adeptly weave these digital threads into tangible success.

## Expanding Your Online Connections

In the digital realm, the importance of expanding your online connections cannot be overstated. As leaders, we are faced with boundaries and opportunities that were unimaginable a few decades ago. Networking in this digital world requires adaptability, strategy, and a keen understanding of the landscape. To truly harness the potential of online connections, one must navigate these waters with purpose and intention.

The first step is understanding that online networks are not just about quantity, but quality. Connections should be meaningful and mutually beneficial. In a hyperconnected space where information flows freely and interactions are frequent, the ability to identify and nurture key relationships can set you apart. It becomes essential to go beyond superficial interactions and invest time in building connections that offer value and resonance.

To foster these connections, you must first establish an authentic online persona. This involves presenting a digital self that resonates with your core values and leadership vision. Crafting an authentic voice requires consistency and transparency, ensuring your online presence aligns with your real-world principles. People are drawn to sincerity—it builds trust, which is the foundation of any meaningful relationship.

While sincerity is crucial, strategic thinking shouldn't be discounted. As you're expanding your online connections, think in terms of influence maps and networks of power. Identify individuals and entities that align with your goals or possess the knowledge, expertise, or access you need. Proactively engaging with them requires more than a simple connection request—it calls for meaningful dialogue. Comment thoughtfully on their work, share insights that demonstrate your understanding, and provide value before you seek value in return.

The tools we use to network are abundant, but none are as powerful as social media platforms. They provide a bridge to countless individuals and communities, offering a stage for leaders to assert their influence. However, successful networking goes beyond merely being present; it demands participation. Engage in discussions, join groups that sharpen your intellect, and offer your expertise. It's not enough to be a member of an online community; you must be an active contributor.

One effective method of expanding your network is through digital collaborations. Identify people whose skills and interests complement yours and propose collaborations that are mutually beneficial. Whether it's co-writing a piece, hosting a joint webinar, or creating content together, collaborations can extend your reach and infuse your network with new ideas and perspectives. Each successful partnership enhances your credibility and widens your circle of influence.

Personal branding is another critical component in the quest to expand online connections. A carefully crafted personal brand not only differentiates you but also attracts like-minded individuals. Share your story, your challenges, and your successes. Let your network see the values you stand for and the expertise you bring to the table. When done effectively, your personal brand becomes a beacon, drawing people who resonate with your vision and are keen to align themselves with you.

However, while expanding your network, it's vital to remain discerning. Not every connection will align with your goals and values. In a digital space rife with information overload and potential distractions, prioritize quality over quantity. Aim for connections that enrich your life and career, not just your follower count. The key lies in curating a network of individuals who support your growth and challenge your thinking.

One shouldn't overlook the significance of maintaining these connections, either. Once initial links are established, the relationship needs nurturing. Regular check-ins, sharing of relevant content, or even a digital coffee chat can keep the connection alive and mutually beneficial. Consistency fosters trust, and over time, these maintained relationships can evolve into genuine partnerships or collaborative allies.

Expanding online connections is also about staying informed and adaptable. Technologies evolve, and so do the platforms and strategies for networking. Be open to new opportunities that arise and continuously seek to learn. Attend virtual conferences, webinars, and forums where new relationships can be forged. In doing so, you ensure your network is not only growing but also evolving with the times.

Furthermore, a global perspective on networking can't be undervalued. Digital tools erase geographical borders, presenting an opportunity to forge connections worldwide. Embrace cultural diversity and seek to understand the nuances of connecting with people from different parts of the world. Being culturally aware not only broadens your perspective but also enhances your ability to lead in diverse environments.

To harness the full potential of these connections, leverage analytics and insights that digital platforms provide. These tools offer valuable information on which networks are thriving and which interactions generate the most impact. By analyzing the data, you can refine your approach, focusing your efforts where they yield the highest returns.

In conclusion, expanding your online connections is an ongoing process that meshes strategic thought with authentic interaction. It's about building a network that supports your aspirations while providing value to others. As you expand your reach, remember that every connection is an opportunity to influence and be influenced, to learn and to teach. In the age of digital leadership, this network is your most treasured asset—nurture it well.

## Building Meaningful Digital Relationships

In today's hyperconnected world, the art of forging meaningful digital relationships stands as a cornerstone of effective leadership. Gone are the days when networking meant handshakes at industry events; now, many of these connections are cultivated in the virtual realm. Just as in Machiavelli's time, where building alliances was critical for gaining and maintaining power, modern leaders must strategically develop and nurture their digital networks.

When crafting digital relationships, the focus should be on authenticity and mutual benefit rather than transactional interactions. In a virtual space, sincerity is often the currency that yields trust. Engaging with others goes beyond liking a post or sending a connection request; it involves meaningful engagement that reflects a genuine interest in the other party's work and achievements. These interactions shouldn't merely be a collection of numbers on a digital platform but rather a tapestry of connections woven with intent and purpose.

Understanding the nuances of digital communication is fundamental. While the written word takes precedence in the digital world, it's important to remember that tone, intent, and personality must still shine through. A leader's communication style should be adaptable yet consistent enough to maintain a cohesive digital presence. Personalizing interactions, even in a broad digital audience, cultivates a sense of belonging and attention that can transform simple exchanges into lasting connections.

Building relationships in the digital landscape also involves the strategic use of social media platforms and professional networks like LinkedIn. Each platform has its unique culture and unwritten rules that dictate how users interact. Leaders should carefully curate their presence across these platforms, ensuring that their digital persona truly reflects their professional values and goals. Participating in relevant discussions, contributing valuable insights, and amplifying others' voices are powerful ways to build rapport and goodwill.

Authenticity doesn't eliminate the need for strategic thinking. To build meaningful digital relationships, modern leaders need to adapt the same strategic thinking that Machiavelli advocated centuries ago. This involves identifying key individuals and groups within the digital sphere whose interests align with theirs. Once these potential allies are identified, leaders should approach with purpose, offering insights, collaboration, or mutual support opportunities.

At the heart of meaningful digital relationships is the concept of reciprocity—a timeless principle of human relationships. Reciprocity fosters a balanced exchange where both parties benefit from the connection. In the digital world, this could mean sharing resources, providing introductions, or offering a platform for others to shine. By giving as much as they take, leaders can cultivate a network teeming with goodwill and trust, essential for navigating the tumultuous waters of digital influence.

Mentorship can play a transformative role in digital relationships. Where traditional mentorship required geographical closeness, digital tools allow mentors and mentees to connect across continents in real time. This boundaryless communication fosters a learning environment enriched by diverse perspectives, which is increasingly valuable in today's globalized dynamic industries. By being open to both receiving and offering guidance, leaders can cement deeper, more genuine connections.

The natural inclination might be to focus on growing a digital network in sheer numbers. However, this isn't always the best approach. It's crucial for leaders to prioritize the depth of their networks over breadth. This means fostering fewer, more meaningful interactions and connections with individuals whose values and goals align. Quality interactions build stronger alliances than any quantity could ever achieve, allowing for a more supportive and collaborative digital ecosystem.

As leaders venture deeper into building their networks, it's vital to remember the importance of diversity and inclusion. A digitally diverse network not only enriches personal growth but also enhances business opportunities by bringing varied viewpoints and insights. Engaging with individuals and communities outside one's usual sphere ensures the network is dynamic and resilient, much like the leaders themselves must be.

Creating meaningful digital relationships also involves a long-term commitment to relationship-building. These connections don't form overnight, and they require nurturing and dedication to flourish. Consistency in engagement and staying true to one's values builds a foundation of trust, making others more eager to maintain a connection. Digital relationships should be viewed as gardens; they thrive when carefully tended with patience and care.

In conclusion, the essence of building meaningful digital relationships lies in the understanding that digital interactions are a natural extension of traditional human connection— adapted for the modern age. By approaching these networks with intent, authenticity, and strategic thinking, leaders can harness the power of digital relationships to not only enhance their leadership journey but also to craft influential bonds that stand strong amidst the relentless tide of digital evolution.

# Chapter 15:
# Strategic Planning for the
# Digital Future

As we stand on the precipice of the digital future, the necessity for strategic planning has never been more critical for leaders wanting to thrive amidst the swirling winds of technological change. Anticipating future trends is akin to possessing a modern oracle, guiding decisions that can either fortify a leader's domain or render it vulnerable to disruptive forces. Embracing a forward-thinking mindset requires not only astute analysis of emerging technologies but also the courage to pivot as new challenges emerge. The leaders of tomorrow will be those who meticulously blend traditional foresight with agile innovation, crafting strategies that are both robust and flexible. By doing so, they pave a course through the unknown, ensuring their influence extends far into the future while deftly sidestepping the pitfalls of digital obsolescence. This strategic foresight will become a linchpin, transforming uncertainty into opportunity and securing a legacy of enduring digital leadership.

## Forecasting Trends

In the digital landscape, the only constant is change—a reality that Machiavelli, were he alive today, would likely embrace with strategic foresight. As leaders navigate this ever-evolving milieu, the ability to anticipate trends becomes paramount. It's about looking beyond the immediate horizon and discerning the trajectories that will shape the future. Such foresight not only empowers leaders to steer their organizations effectively but also positions them as visionaries in a saturated market.

One of the first steps in forecasting trends is developing a keen sense of observation. This involves monitoring the subtle shifts in consumer behavior, technological innovations, and emerging market demands. Leaders must immerse themselves in diverse information sources, from industry reports to grassroots social media movements. It's a delicate balance of parsing reliable data while nurturing an instinct for the qualitative nuances that numbers may not readily reveal.

Moreover, understanding the interplay of global events is crucial. The digital future isn't confined to local or national boundaries; it's a global tapestry of interconnected economies and societies. Observing geopolitical shifts, regulatory changes, and economic fluctuations can offer critical insights into potential trends. While a new technology might be emerging from Silicon Valley, its application and impact may first be realized in a completely different region due to distinct market needs or regulatory landscapes.

However, forecasting isn't merely about data aggregation; it requires critical analysis and the aptitude to connect disparate dots. This capacity for synthesis allows leaders to envisage future scenarios and strategize accordingly. Imagine standing at the crossroads of artificial intelligence, automation, and remote work—a nexus that demands foresight to predict its long-term repercussions on workforce dynamics and industry competition.

In executing strategic foresight, scenario planning emerges as a vital tool. By crafting detailed scenarios based on various potential futures, leaders can prepare for a multitude of outcomes. This approach not only helps in risk mitigation but also fosters innovation by challenging teams to think beyond conventional boundaries. Emphasizing adaptability in these scenarios allows leaders to pivot swiftly as new information becomes available.

An essential element in forecasting is the recognition of disruptive technologies and their ripple effects across industries. Take blockchain, for example. While initially tethered to cryptocurrencies, its potential extends to reshaping sectors like finance, healthcare, and supply chains. Leaders must discern the latent possibilities within such technologies, understanding that today's disruptions often become tomorrow's norms.

Equally important is being attuned to social trends. The evolving expectations of digital citizenship, influenced by factors like privacy concerns and ethical consumption, can redefine market landscapes. As digital users become more discerning, their preferences could drive new business models centered around transparency and accountability. Therefore, leaders should forecast these social dynamics with as much diligence as they would technical innovations.

Implementing effective trend forecasting also requires fostering an organizational culture that values continuous learning and curiosity. By encouraging team members to explore new fields, ideas, and perspectives, leaders cultivate an environment where innovative thinking thrives. This collective foresight acts as a magnifying glass, extending the individual leader's ability to predict and adapt to changing circumstances.

Despite the unpredictability inherent in forecasting, leaders can anchor their strategies in resilience. A resilient approach doesn't merely involve preparing for the best- or worst-case scenarios but focuses on maintaining equilibrium and fluidity amidst uncertainty. Resilient organizations are those that can absorb shocks, reorient themselves quickly, and capture emerging opportunities with agility.

Finally, embracing collaboration can enhance forecasting accuracy and breadth. By combining insights across departments, industries, and even competitors, leaders gain a multi-dimensional view of potential trends. This collaborative approach underscores the importance of networks in our hyperconnected world, where the synthesis of diverse perspectives can lead to more robust and visionary outcomes.

In closing, successful trend forecasting in strategic planning requires a blend of data-driven analysis, creative synthesis, and adaptive execution. It's a journey through complexity, demanding leaders to be both astute analysts and imaginative dreamers. As we stand on the cusp of tomorrow's digital revolutions, the foresight to anticipate and navigate these shifts will distinguish leaders who not only adapt to the future but actively shape it. Machiavelli might have heralded power dynamics of his time, but today's digital leaders must harness the art of forecasting to wield influence in their ever-evolving realms.

## Preparing for Future Challenges

In our rapidly evolving digital landscape, preparing for future challenges isn't just about anticipating what will change—it's about understanding how to navigate change itself. Forward-thinking leaders know that the only constant is change, particularly in a world characterized by technological leaps and shifts in social norms. As we steer our organizations through these digital oceans, embracing uncertainty requires not only strategy but also a mindset rooted in adaptation and resilience.

The first step in preparing for these challenges involves recognizing the signals of impending shifts. Leaders should cultivate an awareness of emerging trends, both within their industry and in seemingly unrelated fields. By keeping a finger on the pulse of technological advancements, socioeconomic shifts, and cultural transformations, they can anticipate disruptions before they occur, rather than reacting only when change is unavoidable.

Moreover, it's crucial that leaders foster a culture of agility within their organizations. This isn't just about flexibility in operations, but about embedding adaptability into the very DNA of their teams. Agile organizations can quickly pivot strategies, reallocate resources, and reassess priorities. This involves cultivating a workforce that's not only skilled but also encouraged to learn continuously and embrace new methods, tools, and perspectives. Empowering employees with a sense of agency and encouraging innovative problem-solving paves the way for more dynamic responses to change.

Leveraging data, while respecting its ethical implications, is another essential strategy for facing future challenges. In the age of big data, making informed decisions is predicated on the ability to harness vast quantities of information efficiently. Leaders must not only embrace data analytics but also discern quality from quantity. This requires investing in advanced analytical tools and fostering expertise within teams to interpret data correctly. However, as we dive deeper into data dependencies, ethical considerations must weigh heavily. Ensuring data privacy and maintaining transparency with stakeholders is not just an ethical obligation but also a critical aspect of trust-building.

The importance of strategic foresight cannot be underestimated in these preparations. Scenario planning, though not a crystal ball, offers a methodical approach to anticipate multiple futures. By preparing for a range of possible scenarios, leaders can develop contingency plans that enable them to respond quickly and effectively no matter what the future brings. This approach smooths the path through uncertainty, helping organizations remain steady in the face of change.

Furthermore, aligning the organization's vision with long-term digital trends ensures relevance and sustainability. As societal and technological landscapes evolve, so too must the mission and goals of any forward-thinking entity. This alignment isn't solely about chasing the latest fads but about a strategic commitment to innovation. It involves reassessing current practices constantly and willing to take calculated risks to stay ahead of the curve.

Building strategic alliances and partnerships is another way to brace for future challenges. In a digital world defined by networks and connections, forming alliances can provide access to new resources, markets, and ideas. These collaborative efforts can enhance innovation and operational efficiencies, offering a competitive edge. Successfully managing partnerships requires clear communication, mutual goals, and a willingness to share both risks and rewards.

Leadership development remains a bedrock in preparing for upcoming challenges. As organizations grow and morph, so too must the skill sets of their leaders. Cultivating leaders with diverse competencies—ranging from technological fluency to emotional intelligence—ensures an organization is well-prepared for the unforeseen. Leadership programs should emphasize adaptability, critical thinking, and creativity, encouraging leaders to be promoters of and participants in a culture of continuous learning.

Cultivating resilience also involves developing robust crisis management strategies that account for the unique challenges of a digital environment. Whether it's responding to cybersecurity threats, managing reputational risks online, or navigating the fallout from digital disruption, leaders need well-rehearsed plans and cross-functional teams trained to respond effectively and swiftly. The goal is to minimize impact while recovering stronger and more informed.

Lastly, embracing a forward-thinking mindset requires a blend of humility and ambition. It's about acknowledging that while the future is unpredictable, preparing for it is a continuous journey. Leaders should strive to inspire their teams, fostering a sense of shared purpose and collective resilience. By doing so, they're not only investing in their organization's future but also ensuring they're poised to turn today's challenges into tomorrow's opportunities.

In essence, the art of preparing for future challenges lies in a leader's ability to blend anticipation with action, adaptability with decisiveness, and vision with pragmatism. This dynamic equilibrium is the key to thriving amidst the shifting sands of the digital future.

# Chapter 16:
# Understanding Global
# Digital Cultures

In a world growing tighter through digital threads, leaders find themselves navigating the intricate tapestry of global digital cultures. The internet's reach demolishes traditional boundaries, ushering in a new era where influence spans continents, resonating through diverse voices and expectations. To lead effectively across this variegated landscape, one must weave through the unique digital imprints each culture leaves online. This requires a nuanced understanding of differing communication styles, values, and digital etiquettes. Modern leaders must foster a flexible mindset, embracing both cultural diversity and commonality. They need to adapt strategies on the fly, showing sensitivity to cultural undercurrents while crafting messages that transcend borders to unite disparate audiences. By respecting these cultural differences, leaders can harness the power of digital platforms to inspire and motivate on a global scale, reinforcing their influence across the digital sphere while adding an indispensable layer of depth and authenticity to their leadership repertoire.

## Leading Across Borders

In the landscape of digital leadership, the ability to lead across borders stands as a transformative skill. As the world becomes ever more interconnected, leaders face the challenge of navigating cultural nuances while driving progress within digital ecosystems. This requires more than just an understanding of different time zones or languages; it demands an appreciation of diverse cultural gestures, social norms, and values that influence behavior and decision-making on the global stage.

Understanding how digital platforms facilitate cross-cultural collaborations is crucial. These platforms have shattered geographical barriers, allowing leaders to communicate seamlessly with team members and stakeholders worldwide. However, this connectivity brings its own set of leadership challenges. Successful leaders will need to interpret and work within this complex web of digital exchanges and cultural subtleties.

To thrive, one must first recognize that each digital interaction can serve as a cultural exchange, laden with implicit expectations and unspoken rules. Consider the way messages are phrased in emails or the timing of responses in instant messages—each element can have different connotations depending on cultural context. A delay in response may be seen as a sign of disrespect in one culture and a reflection of thoughtful consideration in another. These seemingly minor details can have major impacts on global team dynamics.

A leader who can adeptly navigate these waters not only focuses on the words being spoken but also who speaks them, where, and how. The tone, pacing, and even the medium can dramatically alter how messages are perceived. Leaders must become adept at reading between the lines, decoding cultural signals that may not be immediately obvious but are critical to maintaining trust and understanding with their international counterparts.

Furthermore, digital leaders must intentionally learn and respect cultural differences. This means cultivating cultural intelligence—a skill that allows leaders to adjust their style according to cultural expectations and to anticipate how diverse teams might respond to various leadership tactics. It's a strategic blend of curiosity, empathy, and adaptability.

The advantages of such an approach abound. Leaders proficient in cross-cultural digital communication can more effectively mobilize global teams, achieve alignment on strategic objectives, and cultivate an environment where innovation flourishes. The synergy that emerges from a culturally diverse team can drive creativity, offering fresh perspectives that fuel competitive advantage in a crowded marketplace.

However, challenges persist. Even as technology connects us, it can also serve to widen gaps in understanding if not handled with finesse. Miscommunication due to cultural misinterpretations can disrupt workflow, erode trust, and create friction that inhibits progress. The onus is on digital leaders to bridge these gaps proactively. Being culturally agile allows them to anticipate potential conflicts and mitigate issues before they escalate. They must foster dialogues that weave together different perspectives while respecting core cultural tenets.

It's also worth considering the local norms of digital usage and expression across cultures. Platforms like Twitter, LinkedIn, or WhatsApp may serve specific purposes and possess distinct etiquette depending on regional predilections. Familiarity with these nuances augments a leader's capacity to connect authentically, crafting messages that resonate personally and culturally with diverse audiences.

We must also acknowledge the role of cultural syncretism and digital hybridization in shaping modern workplaces. As digital interactions blur the traditional boundaries of work, play, personal, and professional spaces, leaders should facilitate pathways for cultural interexchange and enrichment. This requires fostering an organizational culture that celebrates diversity—not merely as a corporate obligation but as a key driver of innovation and collaboration.

Even as leaders strive for cross-cultural fluency, they must also champion inclusivity. It's vital for digital leaders to recognize and challenge any cultural biases that might exist within their teams or systems. Promoting platforms for open dialogue will help ensure that voices from across the cultural spectrum find equal expression and valuation.

Through initiatives like virtual cultural workshops, regular feedback loops, and fostering an environment of mutual learning, leaders can drive unified goals while respecting the unique contributions each team member brings to the table. This active inclusion fortifies team cohesion and prompts a sense of shared purpose, crucial for achieving long-term success in global contexts.

Finally, leading across borders requires a robust ethical compass. Leaders must be vigilant about navigating ethical dilemmas that can arise from differing cultural norms while adhering to their personal and organizational ethical standards. Walking this tightrope requires diplomacy, an understanding of local realities, and a commitment to integrity and transparency.

In conclusion, leading across borders goes beyond mere coordination and control. It signifies a deep engagement with cultural diversity and the challenges it poses within digital environments. As leaders, it's critical to develop a skill set that does more than connect dots across a map—it bridges worlds, inspires inclusive collaboration, and drives strategic success on a global scale. As we stride forward into this digital century, leaders who can master this art will not only achieve greatness but will redefine its very essence.

## Respecting Cultural Differences Online

In today's fast-paced digital environment, leaders are tasked not only with navigating complex power dynamics but also with bridging cultural divides that transcend geographic borders. The web's global reach means that participants in any conversation or transaction could hail from vastly different cultural backgrounds. For leaders keen on mastering influence and shaping a positive digital presence, respecting and understanding these cultural nuances becomes not just advantageous, but essential.

Consider the notion of time—what some cultures view as a fluid concept, others treat with unyielding precision. In an online meeting, a delay might be customary for one culture, while it could be seen as disrespectful in another. A leader sensitive to these differences will recognize when to adapt their communication style, demonstrating respect and fostering better interactions. This ability to pivot on cultural imperatives can often determine the success or failure of global dealings.

Effective communication across cultural boundaries requires both humility and curiosity. Acknowledging that one's own perspective is not universal opens the door to deeper understanding and meaningful connections. Leaders who excel in this area consistently seek to learn about the cultural contexts of their peers, asking thoughtful questions and showing genuine interest in diverse perspectives. This approach not only builds trust but also lays the groundwork for more collaborative environments.

One might ask: how does a leader prepare to respect cultural differences online? It begins with education. Immersing oneself in the study of global cultures, from reading historical accounts to engaging with international colleagues, equips leaders with the necessary insights to navigate a multicultural digital world. This proactive learning cultivates empathy and enables informed decision-making when cultural sensitivities are in play.

However, understanding cultural differences isn't just about preventing potential faux pas. It opens avenues for innovation and creative problem-solving. When leaders encourage diverse cultural insights within their teams, they unlock a wealth of ideas and perspectives that can drive breakthrough solutions. A team comprised of varied cultural backgrounds is more likely to approach challenges from multiple angles, leading to outcomes that single-minded groups may overlook.

Multicultural digital interactions also present the perfect opportunity to harness the art of active listening. This technique goes beyond merely hearing words, emphasizing the importance of understanding the context, acknowledging unspoken cues, and reading between the lines. In a world where communication is often reduced to text and avatars, leaders must refine their listening skills to identify cultural subtleties and respond aptly.

The digital world offers numerous tools to facilitate cross-cultural respect. Translation applications, while imperfect, provide a starting point for communication. Social media platforms enable a glimpse into cultural expressions and trends. Virtual reality technology offers immersive experiences of different cultures without the need to travel. Forward-thinking leaders leverage these technologies to broaden their cultural awareness.

Yet, as technology brings us closer, it also presents paradoxical challenges. The same tools that connect us can amplify stereotypes if not used judiciously. As such, cultural competence requires a balance of technological savvy and deep personal reflection. Leaders must be vigilant against assumptions and actively counteract misguided representations propagated online. Establishing protocols for inclusive communication can help navigate these pitfalls, ensuring that all voices are heard and valued.

In practice, respecting cultural differences online involves a continual commitment to ethics and sensitivity. Modern leaders must champion inclusivity and equality within their digital spaces. Encouraging dialogues on cultural awareness and implementing policies that respect diverse traditions and customs are critical steps toward inclusive digital environments. These actions not only enrich organizational culture but also reflect positively on brand identity in a globally connected market.

Ultimately, leaders must acknowledge and embrace the transformative power of cultural interaction in the digital realm. By integrating cultural respect into their leadership ethos, they broaden their influence and demonstrate their commitment to fostering diverse voices. In a digital age where leadership paradigms are ever-evolving, the capacity to navigate cultural dynamics is a defining trait of effective leaders. It's a practice anchored in both ancient wisdom and modern strategy, echoing the timeless relevance of adaptability and respect.

The commitment to understanding and respecting cultural differences online is not merely a strategic choice—it's an imperative for anyone looking to lead with influence and integrity in our interconnected world. As we continue to cross digital frontiers, leaders who prioritize cultural respect stand to build stronger relationships, foster innovation, and create a more inclusive global community. In doing so, they not only honor the legacy of past leadership philosophies but also carve out a path for a more equitable digital future.

# Chapter 17:
## Learning from Digital Failures

In the ever-evolving digital landscape, failure isn't just an option—it's a valuable teacher. As leaders venture into uncharted technological territories, missteps are inevitable but not futile. Embracing digital setbacks with an analytical eye reveals miscalculations in strategy or execution, offering an organic curriculum in the school of modern leadership. Each error, whether a misguided campaign or a security breach, carries within it the seeds of understanding and innovation. It's crucial for leaders to dissect these failures meticulously, drawing insights that pave the way for refined strategies and robust recovery plans. By fostering a culture that views missteps as opportunities for growth rather than endpoints, leaders can cultivate resilience and drive continuous improvement. This approach not only aids in repairing the immediate consequences but also fortifies the organization against future disruptions. Ultimately, learning from digital failures transforms potential vulnerabilities into touchstones of progress, reinforcing the fabric of leadership in a world where change is the only constant.

## Analyzing Mistakes

Behind every digital triumph is an unseen tapestry of faltered steps, near-misses, and outright failures. In the shadow of digital victories, one often finds a trail of costly mistakes. However, in the digital age, learning to analyze these mistakes is pivotal for a leader striving to master the art of influence and power. Recognizing the importance of scrutinizing our missteps doesn't just prevent them from happening again; it cultivates a resilient mindset that's essential for navigating today's hyperconnected world.

Mistakes in the digital sphere often manifest in varied forms—overlooking the crucial aspects of user privacy, misjudging a target audience's behavior, or even succumbing to technological myopia. But these are not just isolated errors; they offer insight into the complex web of digital strategies. By dissecting where things went wrong, leaders can extract valuable lessons that contribute to their arsenal of decision-making tools.

Imagine a world where every failure is a learning opportunity. It requires an openness to introspection and a culture of honesty. In the digital realm, this means setting aside time and resources to systematically analyze failures, from botched launches to lost clients. It's about cultivating the humility to admit errors and equipping the team with mechanisms to analyze these errors without fear of reprisal. Such an environment doesn't just recover from mistakes but thrives because of them.

Why is analyzing digital mistakes so significant? Because digital failure is unforgiving—the echo of a misjudged tweet or a failed app feature can reverberate across the globe in seconds. The interconnected nature of digital interactions amplifies both success and failure, meaning that small errors can have outsized consequences. Yet, this amplification also accelerates learning. When mistakes occur, they're spread over vast digital networks, offering immediate feedback and fostering rapid learning cycles.

Consider the power of real-time data and analytics in scrutinizing these failures. Data can reveal hidden patterns and provide actionable insights that wouldn't be apparent through instinctive reflection alone. Leveraging data-driven post-mortems, leaders can quantify the impact of an error and understand its ripple effect across various digital touchpoints. This kind of data-fueled introspection allows for a detailed examination of not just the 'what' but the 'why' behind digital missteps.

Moreover, embracing failure as part of the learning process fosters innovation. Leaders must encourage a culture where experimentation is valued and failure is seen as an indication of bold ventures into the unknown. This directly ties into Machiavelli's teachings adapted for today: exhorting leaders to remain adaptable and resilient, understanding that the path to effective digital leadership is not linear but filled with iterative cycles of trial and error.

In the process of analyzing mistakes, it is crucial to distinguish between technical failures and strategic miscalculations. Technical failures may arise from underestimating the required infrastructure or misaligning technological solutions with business objectives. Meanwhile, strategic miscalculations might root in misunderstanding market demand or misreading cultural nuances across digital platforms. Both require different examination techniques—technical failures may necessitate root cause analysis, while strategic miscalculations benefit from scenario planning and market research breadth.

For digital leaders aiming to master the landscapes of power and influence, acknowledging and learning from mistakes is a strategic imperative. Consider it akin to a natural selection process within your leadership development journey—only by learning and adapting from missteps can your leadership acumen evolve. Mistakes, therefore, should not just be mitigated; they should be honored as a cornerstone of strategic development.

If one can learn from a mistake, it's vital to communicate these lessons throughout the organization transparently. Creating a digital log of lessons learned can serve not only as a deterrent to repeating past mistakes but also as an educational tool for others facing similar challenges. Be it through team discussions or digital forums, sharing experiences encourages a collective advancement that no individual effort ever could.

Leaders who are adept at analyzing mistakes also understand the importance of maintaining a flexible mindset. They remain open to different perspectives and approaches. They listen actively to their teams, valuing their input and making them part of the learning process. It is this inclusivity that empowers diversified thinking, essential when extracting lessons from digital challenges.

Finally, transforming mistakes into lessons requires emotional intelligence and self-awareness. Being a digital leader means possessing the emotional capacity to remain poised when plans derail, and setbacks occur. It involves an awareness of one's weaknesses and the proactive seeking of feedback. This emotional fortitude is what allows leaders to pave their path to recovery, turning temporary setbacks into lasting legacies of success.

In essence, the digital world offers no shortage of opportunities for failure. But within every mistake lies the potential for growth and transformation. By thoroughly analyzing failures with a Machiavellian lens adapted for today's context, leaders not only refine their strategies but also enhance their influence and ability to adapt to future uncertainties. In this light, mistakes become not a roadblock but a stepping stone towards greater leadership efficacy in the digital age.

## Building a Path to Recovery

The digital realm is rife with opportunities for innovation and influence, yet it also harbors significant pitfalls. As leaders navigate this fast-paced environment, the inevitability of failure looms large, not as a mark of incompetence but as a natural checkpoint along the journey. Recognizing that digital failures can be stepping stones, this section delves into how to effectively recover and transform these setbacks into platforms for growth and renewed strength.

In the digital universe, failures brand themselves quickly and broadly. Unlike traditional corporate missteps, digital mishaps are prone to rapid amplification. Consider a software code error or a mistimed social media post; both can spiral into public relations nightmares. Acknowledging the immediacy and breadth of digital failures informs the processes for recovery. The first step is to shift perspective, viewing failures not merely as dead ends but as detours toward greater insight. It's an opportunity to rethink strategies, reinforce weaknesses, and emerge fortified.

Recovery demands a meticulous examination of what went awry. An effective post-mortem is foundational; it dissects every aspect of the failure, revealing blind spots and vulnerabilities. This critical analysis should be precise and devoid of blame— a constructive activity aimed at fortifying future efforts. Imagine an architect poring over blueprints, searching for the structural flaw that caused a collapse. Similarly, digital leaders must scrutinize their systemic approaches, identifying weak links that could compromise integrity.

Once the roots of failure are unearthed, leaders must engage in candid reflection. This involves not just leaders, but their teams, fostering an environment where open dialogues about mistakes become a norm rather than an exception. Creating a culture where failure is acknowledged rather than feared encourages an atmosphere ripe for innovation. Machiavelli himself would argue that true power lies in the ability to adapt and exhibit resilience. Such transparency builds trust, a crucial element in maintaining confidence among stakeholders post-failure.

Bouncing back from a digital failure also requires strategic reparations. Leaders can't just stop at uncovering what went wrong; they must set corrective measures into motion. This involves rebuilding systems, retraining teams, and sometimes even reshaping the entire organizational approach to digital endeavors. Speed is essential here. The digital world rewards the swift, and the quicker an organization can turn a setback into a recovery, the better. Immediate actions to remedy failures showcase decisiveness and commitment to stakeholders, reassuring them of the organization's stability and competence.

Equally vital to immediate recovery is the long-term strategy. Here lies an opportunity for innovation; out of failure comes the necessity for a new direction. Take, for instance, a failed product launch that prompts leaders to rethink their target market or delivery platform. Through an innovative lens, that failure becomes a catalyst for creative solutions, redefining the boundaries of possibility. Embracing failure as a learning tool allows leaders to explore paths previously unseen or considered too risky.

Inherent to the recovery plan is the infusion of resilience into an organization's fabric. Digital leaders must cultivate a mindset that normalizes failure as a component of success. This involves reshaping the narrative around failures, shifting from fatalistic to opportunistic. One way to ingrain resilience is through scenario planning, a future-focused exercise envisioning potential challenges and strategically planning responses. This readiness equips leaders with preemptive problem-solving skills that buffer against future digital upheavals.

Communication is the lifeblood of crisis management. When a digital failure occurs, the initial impulse might be to veer towards damage control through silence; however, proactive communication is a more powerful blow against reputational harm. Engaging with customers, clients, and stakeholders through transparent channels not only demonstrates accountability but also preserves trust. It's about crafting a narrative of honesty and commitment to improvement that reverberates beyond the failure itself.

The lessons garnered from digital failures should be carefully documented and woven into the organization's knowledge base. This repository serves as a reference point for teams, guiding future projects and preventing the recurrence of past mistakes. The resilience that leaders develop can ripple through their teams, empowering everyone to approach future challenges with an enriching mindset that places learning over punishment.

Looking inward, leaders must also view personal growth as an intrinsic part of recovery. The path to recovery is as much about technical fixes as it is about personal resilience and leadership development. Displaying vulnerability as a leader and admitting missteps can humanize those at the helm, fostering solidarity within teams. This internal recovery becomes visible through the renewed vigor and bolstered vision that leaders can impart to their organizations.

In essence, turning a failure into a learning experience requires courage, commitment, and creativity. It's about cultivating an ecosystem where risks are calculable but not paralyzing, and where each digital challenge is met with fervor and fortitude. Indeed, building a path to recovery is about constructing bridges over moments of despair, leading to realms of innovation and enduring success.

# Chapter 18:
## Security Strategies for Digital Leaders

In the rapidly evolving digital world, safeguarding assets and understanding the intricacies of cyber threats have become paramount for modern leaders. Digital leaders must craft a robust security strategy that not only protects vital information but also fortifies the overall resilience of their networks. This involves proactive risk assessment, embracing advanced technologies, and fostering a culture of vigilance within their teams. Leaders today are called to navigate these complexities, as they build fortress-like defenses against ever-evolving cyber threats while maintaining trust and transparency. By doing so, they ensure the integrity and confidentiality of data, which is as much about safeguarding their empire as it is about stewarding future innovations. Machiavelli might remind us that just as fortifications protected kingdoms of the past, so do cybersecurity measures shield the digital realms leaders command today. Armed with the right strategies, digital leaders can strike a balance between openness and protection, ensuring their organizations are prepared to face any challenge head-on.

## Protecting Digital Assests

In the age where bytes and pixels are more valuable than gold and silver, protecting digital assets has become a priority for leaders immersed in the digital realm. The modern leader is often caught in a web of complex networks and systems that require both strategic foresight and immediate tactical responses. To navigate this landscape effectively, digital leaders need to adopt a multifaceted approach to security, one that embraces innovation and champions vigilance. Cybersecurity is no longer a task relegated to IT departments; it is an essential aspect of leadership that permeates every layer of an organization's structure.

A successful strategy for safeguarding digital assets begins with an understanding of vulnerability. Knowledge is indeed power; comprehending the types and sources of threats allows leaders to anticipate and mitigate risks. Cyber threats can range from data breaches and ransomware attacks to malware and phishing scams. These threats aren't just technical issues—they pose significant risks to reputation, customer trust, and ultimately, the bottom line. Thus, keeping abreast of emerging threats and knowing the landscape of digital vulnerabilities is the cornerstone of a robust security strategy.

Leadership in the digital era requires an unwavering commitment to fostering a culture of security. This means embedding cybersecurity at the core of organizational culture and making it a shared responsibility. The collaboration between leadership, IT professionals, and employees creates a unified front against cyber threats. Regular training and awareness campaigns that are engaging and informative help build this collective resilience, transforming employees from potential security risks into the first line of defense.

Deploying advanced security technologies is just as important as cultivating a culture of security. Digital leaders must invest in state-of-the-art cybersecurity tools that monitor, detect, and respond to threats in real time. From firewalls and encryption to intrusion detection systems and multi-factor authentication, these technologies form a digital fortress around valuable assets. However, tools alone aren't enough; leaders must also ensure that these technologies are regularly updated and fine-tuned to address evolving threats.

The concept of defense-in-depth further strengthens digital protections. By layering multiple security measures, organizations can ensure that if one fails, others are in place to neutralize emerging dangers. This approach creates redundancies that discourage attackers while providing multiple lines of defense. It's a strategic methodology that reinforces confidence in the integrity and availability of digital resources.

Digital leaders must not overlook the significance of data privacy in their security strategies. Protecting digital assets involves not only warding off external threats but also safeguarding personal and sensitive information. A leader's role involves adhering to local and international regulations regarding data protection, such as the General Data Protection Regulation (GDPR) and the California Consumer Privacy Act (CCPA). Compliance is a crucial aspect of any security strategy, offering both legal protection and reinforcing trust with stakeholders.

Embracing innovation in security solutions is essential as technology continues to evolve. Artificial intelligence (AI) and machine learning are powerful allies in the fight against cyber threats. These technologies can analyze vast amounts of data to detect patterns indicative of intrusion. They not only enhance threat detection but also provide predictive insights that help preempt attacks. Leaders should be proactive in harnessing these technologies, ensuring their teams are equipped with the knowledge and tools to leverage them effectively.

Incident response planning is another vital component of a comprehensive security strategy. It's not just about prevention—it's about preparing for inevitabilities and responding with agility and confidence. A well-crafted incident response plan outlines roles, responsibilities, and procedures in case of a breach. Regular drills and simulations help teams practice these protocols, reducing panic and ensuring a swift, coordinated response. An effective response plan limits damage, preserves trust, and helps organizations recover more quickly from disruptions.

Furthermore, fostering partnerships with external security experts can enhance an organization's defensive capabilities. Forming alliances with cyber defense firms, participating in security forums, and engaging with ethical hackers for penetration testing are all strategies that can provide additional layers of protection. These partnerships offer access to specialized knowledge and expertise that can be pivotal in preempting and responding to attacks.

Communication, both internal and external, plays a critical role in protecting digital assets. Internally, clear communication ensures that every member of the organization understands security policies and procedures. Externally, transparent communication with customers and stakeholders during a security breach is vital. Honesty in these situations not only mitigates fallout but also rebuilds trust more effectively than attempts to obscure or downplay the extent of a breach.

Digital leaders must also consider the broader implications of geopolitics on cybersecurity. As global tensions impact digital landscapes, being aware of potential nation-state sponsored attacks and understanding the political climate becomes part of the security strategy. Leaders must adopt a global mindset, staying informed and adaptable to shifting international threats that could target their digital assets.

Ultimately, protecting digital assets is about more than just safeguarding information—it's about preserving the integrity, reputation, and ongoing viability of an organization in a digital-first world. The hallmark of effective digital leadership is the ability to anticipate, adapt, and grow stronger in the face of adversities. By applying a strategic balance of technology, culture, and foresight, digital leaders can navigate the complexities of cybersecurity and continue to lead their organizations into the future with confidence and authority.

## Understanding Cyber Threats

In the complex landscape of digital leadership, understanding cyber threats is no longer optional—it's essential. As digital leaders carve out their strategies for influence and power, they must also navigate the turbulent waters of cybersecurity. Cyber threats are not abstract concerns; they're real and present dangers that can undermine even the most well-crafted plans. From phishing schemes aimed at compromising personal information to more sophisticated attacks that target entire infrastructures, the modern digital leader must be vigilant. This vigilance, however, requires more than just knowledge of specific threats; it demands a broad understanding of the intricate web of risks that pervade today's digital environments.

One might equate the cyber landscape to Machiavelli's political battlegrounds—treacherous and constantly evolving. Just as Machiavelli advised rulers to be wary of their adversaries, modern leaders must understand the various forms of cyber threats lurking in the digital realm. These threats don't come with loud warnings or obvious signals; they often lie in wait, silent and invisible, until the moment is ripe. Being prepared isn't just about having the right tools but cultivating a mindset that anticipates potential digital adversities.

The first step in understanding cyber threats is recognizing their diversity. Not all cyber threats are created equal. Some are overt, like ransomware that locks down systems until payments are made. Others are covert, such as malware that quietly infiltrates networks, gathering sensitive data over time. Phishing attacks, for instance, exploit human psychology rather than technological vulnerabilities, crafting seemingly legitimate messages to deceive recipients into revealing sensitive information. Recognizing this variety is the first defense against becoming a victim.

Certainly, the nature of cyber threats is highly dynamic. As technology evolves, so too do the methods of cybercriminals. Today's threat landscape includes advanced methods like "zero-day" attacks, where offenders exploit unknown vulnerabilities in software. These types of threats can be particularly devastating, as they go unnoticed by existing defense mechanisms until damage has already occurred. Yet, technology is also our ally. AI and machine learning contribute to enhanced threat detection and response, offering digital leaders a fighting chance to outpace cybercriminals.

But what's equally critical is the human element. Cybersecurity is often perceived as the realm of IT specialists, but its implications reach team members at every level. Cyber awareness training becomes imperative. Teams must be educated on best practices, equipped to recognize suspicious activities, and empowered to report potential threats effectively. Creating a culture of cybersecurity awareness helps minimize risks and foster collective responsibility in safeguarding digital assets.

Cyber threats can also have significant financial implications. A successful attack can lead to financial loss, whether through direct theft or indirect costs such as business interruptions and reputational damage. Digital leaders need to be proactive in not only understanding these potential economic impacts but also in strategizing ways to mitigate them. This involves budgeting appropriately for cybersecurity measures, investing in robust insurance policies, and preparing comprehensive incident response plans.

Moreover, understanding cyber threats involves recognizing the geopolitical dimensions of cybersecurity. Cyber warfare now plays a significant role in international relations, with state-sponsored attacks becoming a tool for covert aggression. The lines between personal, corporate, and national security have become increasingly blurred, demanding that digital leaders evaluate their defenses within this broader context. Alliances and collaborations with governmental and international bodies might become necessary as they aim to shore up their defenses against these sophisticated operations.

Furthermore, the regulatory environment surrounding cybersecurity is becoming increasingly stringent. Laws and regulations, such as the General Data Protection Regulation (GDPR) in the European Union, mandate specific standards for data protection. Compliance with such regulations is non-negotiable, and failing to adhere can result in significant penalties. Understanding the legal landscape ensures that organizations remain compliant whilst improving their cybersecurity posture.

On a broader scale, there lies the philosophical question: Should cyber threats influence a leader's moral compass? The potential for harm calls into question ethical considerations about data privacy and user consent. Digital leaders are not just tasked with protecting their own domains but must also weigh the broader social implications of their actions and decisions. Integrity becomes an essential facet of leadership in the digital age, as choices made within an organization can ripple outward, affecting broader societal trust in technology.

In the end, understanding cyber threats is an undertaking that demands a strategic blend of awareness, adaptation, and anticipation. Digital leaders must remain abreast of the latest developments in cyber defense technologies while also maintaining a deep understanding of the human factors that influence security. This comprehensive approach prepares leaders not just to respond to threats but to create resilient infrastructures capable of withstanding future challenges.

Leadership in the digital age is, therefore, as much about mastering cyber resiliency as it is about wielding influence and power. By positioning themselves ahead of potential threats, digital leaders not only protect their assets but also reinforce their credibility and authority in the hyperconnected world. Recognizing and understanding cyber threats ensures that their legacy is not defined by breaches and failures but by foresight and fortitude.

# Chapter 19:
# Becoming a Lifelong
# Digital Learner

In an era where technology redraws the boundaries of what's possible almost daily, becoming a lifelong digital learner isn't just beneficial—it's essential. Leaders today must cultivate an insatiable curiosity and embrace online education as a cornerstone for continuous growth. The digital landscape offers a myriad of tools and platforms that, when leveraged creatively, can transform how we learn and lead. By fostering openness to new ideas and skills, leaders can stay ahead of technological advancements, adapting rather than merely reacting to change. This mindset fosters resilience and agility, ensuring that as the digital world evolves, so too does the savvy leader. Such proactive learning is not just about acquiring information but about developing a nuanced understanding of digital transformation—one that equips leaders to navigate and thrive amidst the shifting tides of modernity. Embracing this digital learning journey propels leaders beyond mere survival in the digital age, empowering them to shape the future with confidence and clarity.

## Harnessing Online Education

In today's world, where technology evolves at a rapid pace and reshapes everything it touches, continuous learning becomes not just an advantage but a necessity. For the modern leader, tapping into the vast resources of online education is like unlocking an endlessly evolving toolkit. With a simple click, a leader has access to diverse courses, insightful lectures, and a global pool of knowledge that can be tailored to fit their ambitions. This opens up opportunities not just for personal growth but also for understanding the intricate landscapes in which they operate. With digital resources, one can dive deep into subjects that enhance leadership capabilities like negotiation, data analytics, or even emotional intelligence.

The beauty of online education lies in its flexibility. Gone are the rigid structures of traditional settings; instead, courses can be consumed during a lunch break, during commutes, or even late at night when the world is quiet. This adaptability aligns perfectly with the chaotic schedules of those leading in a digital era. As challenges arise in real-time, so can the solutions—sourced from the reservoir of online knowledge.

But how does one navigate this ocean of options? It starts with a clear identification of personal and professional goals. Whether it's mastering a new coding language or understanding the nuances of digital marketing, clarity in intent ensures your educational journey becomes a direct pathway to real-world applications. Online platforms like Coursera, edX, and LinkedIn Learning offer curated paths for various sectors, but the key is discerning which courses align with your growth ambitions.

Moreover, online education isn't just about hard skills. It's a gateway to understanding cultural nuances and global trends, positioning leaders to think beyond their immediate surroundings. Interactive webinars and virtual workshops expose participants to perspectives from all corners of the globe. This not only broadens understanding but fuels the empathy needed to lead diverse teams effectively.

It's also important to recognize the role of community in online learning. Forums, discussion boards, and virtual study groups play a critical role. They transform solitary undertakings into collaborative efforts, allowing learners to engage, debate, and synthesize new ideas. This communal learning fosters a sense of belonging and solidarity, reassuring leaders they're part of a larger quest for knowledge.

However, digital leaders must also contend with the challenge of maintaining focus amidst endless possibilities. The internet is a double-edged sword, full of distractions as well as knowledge. Time management and disciplined learning schedules can act as guardrails, ensuring productivity does not get lost in the labyrinth of the web.

Incorporating online education into a leader's routine also supports the cultivation of curiosity—the driving force behind innovation and creativity. The modern leader must embrace a mindset that seeks to continuously learn and unlearn, adapting swiftly to a world in perpetual motion. Online educational resources enable leaders to refresh old knowledge while absorbing the new, reinforcing the benefit of being a perpetual student.

Additionally, digital platforms allow leaders to dip their toes into subjects outside their comfort zone, potentially uncovering new passions or useful skills. This cross-disciplinary exploration can yield surprising benefits, fostering innovative thinking by connecting disparate dots across varying fields of knowledge.

Yet, the journey of online education doesn't just end with the consumption of content. Effective leaders must practice and apply what they learn. This practical application solidifies understanding and reveals the true transformative power of education. Leaders who pursue education with an eye toward real-world implementation often find themselves better equipped to lead teams, solve problems, and implement innovative strategies.

As we stand on the precipice of technological evolution, online education serves as a bridge between the present and future. It equips leaders with the skills and insights required to adapt, evolve, and thrive. Embracing this limitless domain is no longer optional; it's imperative for those who wish to lead with foresight and influence in the digital age. Just as Machiavelli once expounded on the virtues of preparation and adaptability in leadership, so too must modern leaders use the vast tools of online education to fortify their leadership prowess.

## Cultivating Curiosity and Openness

The digital age demands more than just technical acuity from modern leaders; it calls for a mindset rooted in curiosity and openness. To navigate this vast, ever-evolving digital landscape, leaders must constantly seek to understand new technologies and emerging trends. Curiosity is the driving force that pushes leaders to question, explore, and innovate, ensuring they don't just keep up with digital advancements, but stay ahead of them.

Gone are the days when leadership success was defined by static knowledge and rigid adherence to conventional strategies. In today's hyperconnected world, the formula for effective leadership is continually transforming. What worked yesterday might not work tomorrow, which is why leaders must cultivate a perpetual state of learning. Curiosity isn't just advantageous—it's indispensable. It ignites a passion for discovery and encourages leaders to delve deeper into the complexities of digital innovations. This embrace of curiosity fosters a culture of continuous improvement, where learning becomes an end in itself, rather than a means to an end.

Openness goes hand in hand with curiosity. It involves being receptive to new ideas, perspectives, and opportunities that the digital world offers. Leaders who practice openness are more likely to embrace change, find value in diverse opinions, and adapt their strategies to align with the fast-paced digital environment. This openness can manifest as a willingness to adopt new technologies or tools, a readiness to pivot in response to data and feedback, or a commitment to transparency in communication.

For Machiavelli-inspired leaders of the digital age, cultivating curiosity and openness requires a conscious effort to move beyond traditional silos. It involves breaking down barriers that hinder the free flow of ideas and fostering an environment where questions are encouraged, and experimentation is the norm. Leaders must not only accept the power of inquiry but must also inspire their teams to question the status quo and think creatively.

Building on Machiavelli's timeless insights about adaptability and flexibility, leaders today can gain a competitive edge by nurturing their teams' inquisitive nature.

In practice, this means creating spaces where diverse voices are heard and valued. This can be achieved through regular brainstorming sessions, cross-departmental collaborations, and open-door policies that encourage the exchange of ideas. By fostering a culture that values curiosity and openness, leaders enable innovation to flourish and team members to contribute their best thinking.

Curiosity drives a leader to embrace lifelong learning. The internet, with its massive repositories of knowledge, offers unprecedented access to information, yet true learning involves more than passive consumption of content. Leaders must be discerning consumers of information, learning not just to intake facts but to synthesize them critically. The art of distinguishing between valuable insights and mere noise is essential. Engaging with varied sources encourages leaders to approach problems from multiple angles and develop well-rounded strategies.

Cultivating curiosity within teams also means investing in professional development and knowledge-sharing initiatives. Online courses, webinars, and digital conferences provide platforms for exploring new skills and ideas. Encouraging team members to share learnings from these experiences enriches the collective knowledge pool. Moreover, peer-to-peer learning opportunities harness the power of shared experiences, allowing team members to learn from each other's successes and challenges.

Openness is equally vital in building trust and credibility in digital interactions. Transparent communication builds confidence among stakeholders, and leaders who remain open about their intentions and thought processes earn loyalty and respect. In digital spaces, where information can be easily misrepresented or misunderstood, practicing open communication reduces ambiguity and enhances relationships.

Moreover, openness involves recognizing and celebrating the diversity of voices in global digital cultures. Today's leaders must be willing to learn from other cultures, regions, and industries. Exposure to diverse viewpoints not only enriches personal perspectives but also leads to innovative solutions that might otherwise remain undiscovered. This cultural openness ensures that leaders can operate effectively in a globalized world, respecting and leveraging the varied experiences of people across digital networks.

As digital leaders cultivate an environment of curiosity and openness, they also prepare themselves to face unforeseen challenges with resilience. New technologies and digital platforms often arise unpredictably, disrupting established systems. A curious mind is better equipped to approach these disruptions with agility, viewing them as opportunities for growth rather than obstacles. Openness allows leaders to be adaptable and responsive in the face of rapid change, ensuring that they lead with confidence and clarity.

To instill curiosity and openness as core values, leaders must model these behaviors themselves. Leading by example in exploring new ideas and engaging in open dialogue sets a precedent for their teams. When leaders share their learning journeys, admit their uncertainties, and show enthusiasm for discovery, they cultivate a culture where curiosity and openness become the norm. This inspires others to engage with the world in meaningful and innovative ways.

The intersection of curiosity and openness forms the bedrock of effective digital leadership today. It empowers leaders to be continuous learners, skilled communicators, and inclusive collaborators. In this dynamic environment, leaders can't afford to rest on their laurels; they must continually question, explore, and adapt, keeping their organizations agile and forward-thinking.

Cultivating curiosity and openness isn't merely an abstract strategy—it's a practical approach that modern leaders utilize to harness their full potential and the collective potential of their teams in the digital age. By embedding these values into their leadership style, leaders not only navigate the complexities of the digital realm with greater ease but also pave the way for a future rich with innovation and progress.

# Chapter 20:
# Inspiring Digital Citizenship

In a world where screens mediate our every move, inspiring digital citizenship becomes more than a mere duty; it's a powerful strategy towards sustainable leadership. Modern leaders, echoing Machiavelli's wisdom, must now champion the principles of responsible technology use, fostering environments where digital streets are navigated with care and ethical consideration. The art of leading online goes beyond conducting oneself with integrity; it calls for setting an inspiring example, one that encourages others to act with similar integrity and purpose. By exhibiting transparency and promoting healthy digital habits, leaders can cultivate communities that are not only engaging but are deeply rooted in respect and accountability. In these spaces, every click, share, and like carries the weight of influence, offering leaders a profound opportunity to mold the future of digital society—a task as challenging as it is vital. The journey of nurturing this modern digital citizenship requires patience and vision, urging leaders to think beyond traditional power dynamics and towards a world where ethical digital engagement becomes the norm.

## Encouraging Responsible Use

In the digital age where connections are instantaneous and information flows seamlessly, the essence of digital citizenship cannot be overstated. We've navigated through the intricacies of power dynamics, persuasion, ethics, and decision-making, all integral skills for today's digital leaders. Now, we arrive at the heart of responsible use—an aspect deeply woven into the fabric of digital citizenship, urging leaders to wield their influence with integrity and purpose.

The digital realm offers boundless opportunities but equally presents unique challenges that modern leaders need to address responsibly. Responsible use extends beyond mere adherence to rules and protocols; it's about fostering a culture that encourages ethical behavior, respect, and accountability online. As leaders, how can we champion a world where technology amplifies our best qualities rather than our worst? The answer lies in commitment—to understanding, implementing, and nurturing principles of responsible use across all digital landscapes.

One of the fundamental aspects of digital citizenship is the ability to discern the impact of our actions and words in the virtual space. In encouraging responsible use, leaders should prioritize teaching and modeling how individual actions contribute to broader societal norms. It's about recognizing the power of one's digital footprint and ensuring that it contributes positively to the communal digital experience. Constructive engagement means advocating for transparency, nurturing a culture of respect in interactions, and emphasizing the value of authenticity in all digital communications.

Encouraging responsible use also involves a nuanced understanding of the platforms and tools we leverage. It's about striking a balance between innovation and ethics.

Technology, powerful as it is, can be a double-edged sword. Leaders should guide others in using digital tools for empowerment, not exploitation. This includes implementing practices that prevent misinformation, cyberbullying, and data breaches. By fostering an environment where integrity is paramount, leaders ensure that digital spaces are safer and more inclusive for all.

Moreover, responsible use calls for a proactive stance on privacy and security. Leaders must advocate for robust policies that protect user data, encouraging a culture where privacy is a right, not a privilege. This involves understanding the implications of data sharing, informed consent, and the ethical boundaries of surveillance. Encouraging responsible use means holding conversations about when and how data should be used, ensuring that technologies serve humanity rather than compromise it.

To cultivate a culture of responsible use, education is key. Leaders must become educators and mentors, imparting knowledge and frameworks that empower individuals to think critically about their digital interactions. Whether it's through structured training programs or informal mentoring, the goal is to elevate the consciousness of all digital citizens regarding their roles and responsibilities within the digital ecosystem. The more informed and aware individuals are, the more likely they are to engage responsibly.

Inspiring digital citizenship through responsible use also means adapting to our ever-evolving technological landscape. As new technologies emerge, from AI to blockchain, leaders must guide their communities in understanding the ethical implications and potential societal impacts. This forward-thinking approach prepares organizations to not only adopt technological advancements but also to harness them responsibly and for the greater good.

Thus, the ethos of responsible use should be reflected in organizational culture and values. Leaders should ensure that their digital strategies align with ethical principles, fostering a mindset where success is measured not just by metrics but by the positive influence and integrity exhibited in digital spaces. This involves creating policies that support ethical behaviors, recognizing and rewarding those who exemplify responsible use, and continuously refining these policies to adapt to new challenges.

Creating a culture of responsible use isn't a solo endeavor; it thrives through collaboration and collective effort. Leaders should cultivate partnerships with other organizations, communities, and stakeholders to promote shared values and objectives. By leveraging the collective power of multiple voices, leaders can influence broader societal changes and contribute to forging a digital future rooted in ethical use and mutual respect.

Encouraging responsible use is also about leading by example. Leaders set the tone for what is acceptable and expected in digital engagements. When leaders embrace responsibility in their own digital interactions, they inspire others to follow suit. This modeling behavior demonstrates the critical role of character and principle in digital leadership, reminding individuals that every interaction is an opportunity to reinforce a culture of respect and accountability.

In conclusion, embracing the mantle of encouraging responsible use is a vital step toward inspiring digital citizenship. As we've explored, it involves a multifaceted approach—embedding ethics in technology use, fostering education and awareness, and modeling integrity in every action. It's a commitment to shaping a digital world where technology elevates, empowers, and respects human dignity. By focusing on responsible use, leaders not only inspire others but also ensure that the digital future is a reflection of our highest values and aspirations.

## Leading by Example Online

As influencers, leaders, and role models in today's digital age, the concept of leading by example has never been more critical. The online world presents a unique stage where actions speak louder than words, and every keystroke can carry significant weight. In a realm where attention is fragmented and quickly shifting, consistently demonstrating positive digital behavior can profoundly impact both immediate circles and broader communities. Effective digital leaders understand that they are constantly under scrutiny, and their online engagement sets a standard others will follow.

In the past, leadership often revolved around direct interactions, face-to-face meetings, and the conventional office hierarchy. Today, much of that influence is exerted through digital platforms, where a single tweet, post, or comment can cascade through networks. Navigating these platforms with integrity and purpose doesn't just enhance a leader's reputation—it also fosters an environment where positive digital citizenship can flourish. The ripple effect of such practices extends far beyond immediate followers, influencing broader digital societies.

One crucial aspect of leading by example online is the practice of transparency. Leaders thrive when they communicate authentically and openly share their journeys, challenges, and triumphs. This transparency builds trust, an invaluable currency in a virtual world where skepticism can reign supreme. By admitting mistakes, acknowledging uncertainties, and highlighting learning moments, leaders humanize their digital personas, encouraging others to act similarly.

It's equally important to maintain a consistent voice and vision across digital platforms. Leaders who demonstrate determined purpose and coherent messaging create a sense of reliability in a space often marked by chaos and confusion. This coherence provides followers with a compass by which to navigate their own digital experiences, promoting a sense of intentional community. For leaders, every interaction is an opportunity to reinforce their values and demonstrate resilience in the face of challenges inherent in digital landscapes.

Responsible engagement also involves recognizing the darker facets of digital platforms and actively working against them. Trolls, misinformation, and divisive content attempt to fragment communities and sow discord. By taking a firm stand against such negative elements, leaders can set a precedent for constructive and inclusive dialogue. This doesn't mean evading controversy or avoiding difficult conversations, but rather addressing them with civility, reason, and respect.

Encouraging collaboration and amplifying diverse voices is another vital component of leading by example online. Whether through retweets, shares, or highlighted discussions, showcasing a variety of perspectives offers a well-rounded view of the issues at hand. Leaders go beyond self-promotion and cultivate an ecosystem where everyone feels empowered to contribute. This inclusivity can uplift marginalized voices and create a more balanced digital narrative.

Moreover, leaders who exemplify a commitment to learning and growing publicly inspire others to do the same. The digital world offers vast resources for personal and professional growth; leaders who eagerly engage with new technologies, platforms, and ideas model the importance of lifelong learning. By sharing insights, leaders not only broaden their horizons but also encourage followers to embark on their own journeys of discovery, fostering a culture of curiosity and innovation.

At the heart of successful digital leadership lies empathy and kindness. The anonymity and distance of online interactions can sometimes strip away our humanity. Yet leaders who consistently demonstrate understanding, patience, and generosity set an indelible tone for their networks. Practicing empathy online may require effort but ultimately cultivates a safer, more responsive, and harmonious digital environment.

Finally, digital leaders understand the power of digital storytelling in inspiring others. Stories have always been a fundamental tool for shaping culture and values, and the digital arena is no different. Leaders proficient in weaving narratives turn complex concepts into compelling, relatable messages. These stories can resonate across digital channels, motivating individuals to reflect on their own practices and values.

Navigating the intricacies of the digital world necessitates a blend of vigilance, adaptability, and intentional practice. Leaders must remain aware of emerging trends, adapt to quickly evolving platforms, and ensure their actions consistently reflect their core values. By doing so, they create sustainable models of leadership that others can emulate. Leading by example online is less about telling others how to act and more about embodying principles that gradually transform digital spaces into places of growth, collaboration, and respect.

# Chapter 21:
# The Evolution of Authority
# in a Digital World

In today's digital landscape, the concept of authority is undergoing a seismic shift. Traditional hierarchies are giving way to dynamic networks where influence is fluid and multifaceted. This transformation demands leaders who can adapt to new power structures, where authority isn't merely bestowed by title but earned through the ability to navigate and harness digital connectivity. As the rigid, vertical chains of command dissolve, modern leaders must become adept at understanding the nuanced web of relationships that define the digital age. Successful leadership now hinges on the capacity to engage with diverse communities, leverage real-time data, and foster environments of collaboration and transparency. To stay relevant, leaders need to constantly redefine their roles, balancing the need for control with the empowerment of others, and embracing the unpredictability of an interconnected world. The evolution in authority is not just a change in structure but a transformative journey that demands a new mindset, capable of seizing opportunities in a landscape where information flows freely and boundaries are ever-expanding.

## From Hierarchies to Networks

In the era of digital transformation, authority no longer flows from the top down but radiates outward through dynamic networks. Hierarchies, once the cornerstones of structured leadership and power distribution, are now giving way to fluid networks that thrive on connectivity and collaboration. This transition is more than a mere organizational shift; it represents a fundamental evolution in how influence is wielded and alliances are forged.

To understand this transformation, one must first grasp the essence of a network. Networks operate on principles of decentralization, empowerment, and shared knowledge. They mirror the very structure of the internet: an interconnected web where information travels not along a linear path, but in a dynamic dance of nodes interlinked in real-time. In stark contrast to the rigid top-down systems of traditional hierarchies, networks are adaptive, responsive, and inherently collaborative.

Traditional power structures focus on control and command, where authority is often tied to one's position within a strict corporate ladder or bureaucratic framework. This model, while effective during the industrial age, becomes less applicable when faced with the rapid changes and unpredictable nature of the digital realm. Today, influence is garnered not by titles but by visibility, interactions, and the ability to engage a community of followers or peers.

The network model proves its value especially in the age of social media. Leaders who adapt thrive by engaging actively with their stakeholders—be it employees, customers, or the public. Platforms like Twitter, LinkedIn, and Instagram have transformed ordinary individuals into influencers whose voices carry weight. The ability to leverage these digital platforms effectively serves as a testament to a leader's understanding of networked authority.

Why does this transition from hierarchies to networks matter for modern leaders? It's because the very nature of influence has fragmented across various channels. Success in this environment depends on one's ability to navigate and influence these networks to drive change and innovation. Leaders must develop a skill set that transcends traditional management methodologies. This includes the ability to listen actively, communicate authentically, and build trust within diverse digital ecosystems.

The shift to networks doesn't imply that hierarchies are obsolete. Rather, the most successful leaders integrate the beneficial aspects of both models. They establish flexible structures that allow for empowerment and organic growth while maintaining clarity of vision and purpose. It's about striking a balance between fostering freedom and maintaining alignment, a task easier said than done but crucial in sustaining organizational health and resilience.

Furthermore, networks empower leaders to harness collective intelligence—a mosaic of perspectives, skills, and insights. In this decentralized framework, decision-making becomes more democratic and inclusive, enhancing not only the speed of execution but also the quality of outcomes. When a leader taps into the crowd's collective wisdom, they can navigate complexities with more agility and innovation.

One of the profound lessons from this shift is the importance of adaptability. Leaders who are agile in their approach are more effective in managing uncertainty and leveraging new opportunities. They recognize that in a networked world, the landscape is ever-morphing, and the rules continually change. Those who embrace continuous learning and foster an environment of perpetual curiosity are better equipped to lead from the front.

A fascinating case in point is the rise of open-source communities. These self-organized groups illustrate how effective networked collaborations can be. Without formal hierarchies, they manage to successfully create, innovate, and distribute software that powers businesses and governments alike. The Linux operating system and the collaborative projects on GitHub represent the power of networks in action, devoid of constraints imposed by traditional hierarchies.

The challenge for leaders today is to nurture their organizations to think and operate like networks. This means cultivating an environment ripe for experimentation, risk-taking, and unconventional thinking. Leaders should encourage cross-functional collaborations and dismantle silos that inhibit the free flow of information. By doing so, they align organizational goals with the natural pulse of these digital ecosystems, ensuring relevance and competitive advantage.

As we navigate this digital age, the question for leaders isn't whether to adapt but how swiftly and effectively they can integrate networked authority into their leadership style. Embracing the ethos of networks requires a shift in mindset from ownership of resources to access and influence. It's about building the right connections, alliances, and partnerships that extend beyond organizational boundaries.

In conclusion, the evolution from hierarchies to networks represents a seismic shift in leadership dynamics, one that demands both strategic foresight and emotional intelligence. By understanding and embracing the principles of networks, leaders can not only thrive in this new world but also shape its future. This transition empowers leaders to redefine how they lead, how they influence, and ultimately, how they leave a lasting impact on the digital landscape.

## Redefining Leadership Roles

As we continue to explore the evolution of authority in our increasingly digital world, it becomes apparent that traditional concepts of leadership are undergoing significant transformations. Authority is no longer conferred through hierarchical structures alone; it's being reimagined in a dynamic blend of influence, relationships, and agility. The shifting landscape demands a critical rethink of leadership roles, and the traits that define a successful leader.

Traditionally, leadership was synonymous with power and control — those at the top made decisions cascading down through layers of middle management. However, in the digital age, such linear approaches often clash with the fluid and decentralized nature of digital networks. Today, leadership is less about command and more about collaboration. The modern leader must adapt to flatter organizational structures, where teams are empowered to make agile decisions and foster innovation from the ground up. This shift demands leaders who aren't just skilled strategists but also empathetic facilitators who can harness the collective intelligence of their teams.

The digital leader of today must also embrace the role of a connector. In a world characterized by vast networks and constant information flow, leaders need to build bridges both within and outside their organizations. They must nurture external partnerships while facilitating internal cohesion. Success hinges on the ability to weave a tapestry of diverse perspectives, technologies, and cultures into a coherent vision that capabilities across various domains can rally around.

Imagine a CEO in the fast-paced tech sector who relies not only on their internal team but also on open-source contributions, partnerships with startups, and feedback from online communities. Such a leader acts as a conductor, harmonizing these elements to drive innovation and competitive advantage. This role requires a nuanced understanding of digital ecosystems and an openness to new, sometimes unconventional, forms of collaboration.

Moreover, in redefining leadership roles, the focus has shifted toward a more human-centric approach. Emotional intelligence is as critical as technical savvy. Leaders must demonstrate empathy and authenticity to build trust and commitment among their teams. By placing a premium on these qualities, leaders can foster environments where creativity and innovation thrive, and where team members feel valued and motivated.

Yet, it's not enough to be empathetic and collaborative. In the digital age, a successful leader must also be a perpetual learner. With technology evolving at breakneck speed, leaders need to continuously update their knowledge and skills. This involves not only staying abreast of technological advancements but also understanding their implications on their teams and industry. The old adage of "leadership by example" holds true; leaders who embody a culture of lifelong learning inspire their teams to do the same.

Consider the disruptive impact of artificial intelligence (AI) and automation on traditional job roles. Leaders must proactively engage with these technologies, both in understanding their potential and in addressing the anxieties they create among employees. By openly discussing the changes and providing support for skills development, leaders can mitigate fears and facilitate smoother transitions within their teams.

The nature of feedback and assessment is another area undergoing redefinition. Traditional annual performance reviews are gradually being replaced by continuous feedback mechanisms. In an environment where agility is key, leaders must adopt real-time evaluation approaches, making use of digital tools to offer prompt, actionable insights. This approach not only ensures alignment with goals and values but also empowers team members to adapt swiftly and improve.

In parallel, the digital environment necessitates that leaders also redefine how they perceive failure. Failure in the digital age isn't merely an outcome to be avoided; it's a critical part of the innovation process. Modern leaders must champion a culture where calculated risks are rewarded and failures are dissected for the insights they offer, driving learning and growth.

Furthermore, as digital transformation blurs the lines between the personal and professional realms, leaders must also redefine boundaries in their own roles. They need to strike a balance between the demands of a hyperconnected world and the necessity of personal well-being. Demonstrating the importance of work-life balance and mental health sets a powerful example and creates healthier, more sustainable working environments for their teams.

Ultimately, redefining leadership roles in the digital era involves embracing a mindset of adaptability and openness. It's about relinquishing control in favor of inspiring and empowering others. Leaders must craft narratives that resonate and motivate, while also standing as beacons of ethical behavior and transparent decision-making. These narratives should not only inspire those within their immediate organization but also influence broader societal discourse.

In conclusion, the task of redefining leadership roles in a digital world is as challenging as it is rewarding. It calls for leaders who are multifaceted — simultaneously strategists, collaborators, learners, and humanists. As authority in the digital age continues to evolve, those who lead effectively will be those who can blend timeless principles of leadership with modern innovations, fostering environments that not only adapt to change but also anticipate and drive it. By embracing this redefinition, leaders not only prepare their organizations for the future but also equip themselves to thrive in it, ultimately cementing their legacy in an era defined by rapid change and boundless opportunity.

# Chapter 22:
# The Intersection of
# Technology and Humanity

As we journey deeper into the digital age, leaders face the profound challenge of harmonizing the relentless march of technology with the timeless qualities that define our humanity. This intersection is not a mere crossroads but a transformative landscape requiring a delicate dance between innovation and empathy. Leaders who master this balance don't just leverage technology; they ensure it remains subservient to the human spirit, prioritizing the enhancement of human connection, ethical reasoning, and purpose-driven initiatives. The key lies in using technology as a tool to augment human potential rather than replace it, fostering environments where creativity thrives within structured digital frameworks. In doing so, leaders create a synergy that can propel humanity toward a future where technology serves as an enabler for more meaningful interactions and deeper understanding, crafting a world where progress is measured by the well-being of people, not just technological advancements.

## Balancing Humanity with Innovation

In a world where technology is constantly reshaping the landscape of leadership, the challenge remains to balance this innovation with the innate qualities that make us human. It's a delicate dance between embracing the relentless march of progress and nurturing the empathy, creativity, and ethical grounding that define our humanity. Navigating this balance requires leaders to possess not only technical prowess but also a profound understanding of human nature. The essence of this chapter is to equip leaders with strategies that ensure technology serves humanity, rather than the other way around.

At the heart of this balance lies the understanding that while technology can enhance efficiency, it is never a substitute for genuine human connection. Human emotions, creativity, and moral judgment cannot be entirely replicated by algorithms or machines, no matter how advanced. As the digital world rapidly evolves, strategic leaders are those who can wield technological tools without losing sight of their intrinsic values and ethical compass. They recognize that their decisions impact not only organizational outcomes but also the well-being of their teams and communities.

The modern leader's task is thus to integrate technological advancements in ways that augment human capabilities and foster an environment where people feel valued and inspired. This requires creating spaces where innovation thrives alongside human creativity. Leaders must cultivate a culture that encourages exploration and experimentation, while also recognizing and rewarding the unique strengths that individuals bring to the table. This means not only leveraging data and analytics for informed decision-making but also valuing the intuition and experience that only humans can provide.

In practical terms, balancing humanity with innovation involves fostering an organizational culture that prioritizes meaningful interactions. Leaders should strive to build teams that reflect diversity in thought and experience, ensuring that technology serves as a bridge rather than a barrier. By weaving an organizational tapestry that values both technological advancement and human connection, leaders can ensure that employees are engaged and motivated, leading to improved productivity and satisfaction.

Moreover, it's essential for leaders to remain vigilant against the dehumanizing potential of technology. Automating processes and workflows can be a double-edged sword, offering significant efficiency gains but also posing risks of alienation among team members. Therefore, maintaining a human touch is critical. Regular face-to-face interactions, even in a virtual setting, help maintain team cohesion and nurture an ethos of collaboration. Leaders should leverage digital tools to enhance communication but never to replace the nuances of in-person interaction completely.

As automation and artificial intelligence (AI) become more integrated into everyday business operations, stakeholders may worry about the implications on employment and value creation. Enlightened leaders address these concerns by ensuring that technology acts in the service of humanity, not as its adversary. This involves thoughtful deployment of AI and automation—those that complement and expand human roles rather than replace them. By retraining and upskilling their workforce, leaders can tap into the transformational power of technology without disregarding the human element.

Another key aspect of balancing humanity with innovation is ethical leadership. It involves acknowledging and navigating the ethical dilemmas associated with technological progress. Leaders are increasingly called upon to evaluate the moral implications of their tech-driven decisions, from data privacy and surveillance to the equitable distribution of technological benefits. It's vital for leaders to not only comply with regulations but also go beyond them by developing corporate policy frameworks that prioritize ethical considerations in every aspect.

Transparency becomes a non-negotiable tenet in this landscape. Leaders must engage in open conversations about the potential impacts of new technologies, fostering an atmosphere of trust and inclusion. This empowers employees and stakeholders to voice their concerns and aspirations, effectively piercing the veil of technological complexity. An organization thriving on transparency will inherently cultivate loyalty and respect, allowing for sustained growth and innovation.

Through the articulation of a clear ethical vision that incorporates the equitable and responsible use of technology, leaders pave the way for a future where innovation doesn't come at the expense of humanity. They demonstrate that it is possible to harness the power of technology for social good, addressing societal challenges while maintaining profitable operations. This delicate balance is foundational to maintaining not only organizational success but also societal trust.

Ultimately, balancing humanity with innovation demands leaders who are not only technologically savvy but also deeply empathetic. They must be advocates of continuous learning, continually updating their knowledge and adapting to new realities. Such leaders value the human contributions to problem-solving and decision-making, which cannot be replicated by machines. By preserving the human touch while navigating technological advancement, leaders can ensure that they remain relevant and effective in a world that is rapidly transforming. For it is in the fusion of cutting-edge technology with the timeless principles of human insight and compassion that true progress resides.

## Ensuring Technology Serves People

In today's fast-paced digital world, the important question isn't just whether technology can do something, but rather, should it. Technology should be viewed not as an end but as a means to achieving a more equitable and connected world. This brings us to a crucial point in our exploration of technology's role in society: ensuring it serves humanity rather than the other way around.

Many leaders find themselves caught in the overwhelming tide of innovation. With every new gadget, app, or platform promising unprecedented convenience or profitability, there's a constant seduction to adopt technology for technology's sake. Yet, the essence of true leadership in the digital era lies in strategically selecting which technologies to embrace. Leaders must focus on those technologies that empower people, enhance their capabilities, and foster genuine connections.

Balancing human needs with technological advances calls for foresight and ethical consideration. It's easy to be swept up in the marvels of what modern tech can achieve. But it's crucial to remember that technology is merely a tool, and its utility is only as moral as the hands that wield it. Leaders must be proactive in employing technology to bridge gaps, enhance learning, and promote well-being. They should cultivate a mindset that questions and challenges the ethical implications of new tech, advocating for those innovations that genuinely uplift and unify societies.

Consider the realm of artificial intelligence and automation. These advancements hold the potential to revolutionize industries and improve efficiency, but they also pose significant challenges. They can displace jobs, create inequalities, and even exacerbate socio-economic divides. Leaders must navigate these waters with a careful hand, ensuring that AI and automation are deployed in a manner that supports rather than undermines the workforce. This might mean advocating for policies that promote retraining and upskilling, ensuring that workers are prepared for the jobs of the future.

Moreover, the integration of technology should be viewed through the lens of enhancing human interaction and relationships. In our highly connected world, technology should support personal connections rather than alienate individuals. The social media platforms, communication tools, and virtual realities leaders choose to champion should facilitate meaningful engagement rather than superficial exchanges. This conscious selection of technology will help ensure it serves a unifying role, promoting understanding across cultures and communities.

The most compelling leaders today are those who intuitively understand the narrative power of technology. They recognize its ability to amplify voices and bring to the forefront stories that might otherwise go unheard. These leaders cultivate an environment where technology is used to bolster diverse perspectives, inviting dialogue and encouraging collaboration across the digital landscape. They are committed to creating a digital world that's inclusive, where technology is a democratizing force that levels playing fields and advances social justice.

Yet, serving people through technology doesn't merely involve choosing the right tools. It also requires fostering an environment of trust and transparency. In an age where data collection is ubiquitous, and privacy concerns abound, leaders must advocate for responsible use of information and robust data protections. Trust is a pivotal currency in the digital age. Leaders who can handle personal data with integrity, providing users with clear, truthfully articulated choices about how their data is used, will foster loyalty and inspire others to follow their example.

It's vital for leaders to set a strong example, demonstrating how technology can enhance rather than hinder human potential. This involves prioritizing tech-literacy and education, ensuring individuals have the knowledge and skills to navigate an increasingly tech-dependent world. Leaders might champion educational initiatives that teach coding, digital ethics, and critical thinking in tech, ensuring future generations are empowered and prepared to wield technology responsibly.

Technology that serves people also means supporting mental wellbeing in the digital age. The constant hum of digital connectivity can lead to burnout and stress, as the lines between work and leisure blur. Leaders should promote a balanced relationship with technology by encouraging digital detoxes, mindfulness practices, and setting healthy digital boundaries. By doing so, they help cultivate a more resilient and well-rounded workforce that can leverage technology without being overwhelmed by it.

In conclusion, ensuring technology serves people is about more than just keeping pace with innovation—it's about curating a future where technology amplifies the human experience instead of overshadowing it. Leaders in the digital age must wield their influence wisely, aligning technological advances with core human values and needs. By embracing strategies that prioritize the well-being, empowerment, and unity of people, they can ensure that technology fulfills its true potential as a servant of humanity, not its master.

This approach to digital leadership not only aligns with Machiavelli's pragmatic outlook on power but also brings a thoughtful, human-centric perspective to navigating our complex, technological world. As digital leaders, crafting a future where empowering people stands at the forefront of every technological decision will ensure progress doesn't come at the expense of our humanity.

# Chapter 23:
# The Future of Digital Leadership

As we peer into the horizon of digital leadership, the landscape brims with uncharted territories defined by emerging technologies and unprecedented connectivity. The next generation of leaders must hone their foresight to navigate this transformative epoch, recognizing that adaptability and vision are their greatest allies. With technological innovations like artificial intelligence, blockchain, and quantum computing poised to reshape power structures, the traditional paradigms of leadership will inevitably evolve. Leaders must cultivate a mindset that embraces change, pairing Machiavellian strategy with an ethos of ethical stewardship. The art of digital leadership will become a delicate balance between harnessing cutting-edge tools and preserving human-centric values. By fostering dynamic networks and encouraging cross-disciplinary collaboration, future leaders will not just adapt to the digital age but will actively shape its course, crafting new paradigms where agility and empathy merge into powerful, transformative leadership. The future beckons those willing to rethink what leadership can become in this ever-accelerating digital realm.

## Preparing for Emerging Technologies

As we stand on the brink of a technological transformation, the landscape of leadership is evolving in ways that could have been barely imagined just a decade ago. Preparing for emerging technologies is not just a necessity; it's an imperative for any leader wishing to thrive in tomorrow's digital realm. Today's leaders must not only anticipate technological advancements but also leverage them to their advantage. To do so requires an understanding of both technological trends and the foundational principles of leadership that remain timeless.

Emerging technologies, such as artificial intelligence, blockchain, and the Internet of Things, are reshaping industries and altering the interplay of power and influence. Leaders must develop an adaptive mindset to harness the potential of these technologies while mitigating their associated risks. It's not just about adopting new tools; effective leadership requires a strategic vision that integrates technology with organizational goals, leading innovations in a way that aligns with the overall mission.

The pressure to stay ahead can be daunting, but it is crucial to adopt a proactive stance on learning and innovation. Leaders must engage in continuous education, exploring how these technologies can revolutionize processes and redefine competition. One approach involves building interdisciplinary teams that combine technological expertise with strategic insight, fostering an environment where experimentation is encouraged and failure is viewed as part of the learning curve.

This constant evolution challenges leaders to rethink their roles. They must transition from being decision-makers to becoming facilitators of collaboration and architects of ecosystems that span various technological landscapes. Leaders in the digital age are not just anticipating what's next; they are actively shaping it. They understand that the key to leadership in this new era is not just about navigating the unknown but also about embracing it, seizing opportunities that technology presents while ensuring that they remain grounded in human values.

Navigating these changes also requires a shift in perspective towards ethical leadership. With technologies like AI raising questions about privacy, autonomy, and bias, leaders must champion ethical standards and transparency. Leaders are now tasked with not only ensuring compliance but fostering a culture where technology is used responsibly and sustainably, respecting human rights and diversity.

Forward-thinking leaders will prioritize the development of digital literacy within their organizations, recognizing that technology is only as effective as the people using it. By investing in training and development, they equip their teams with the skills needed to leverage new tools, fostering a culture of continuous improvement and innovation. Moreover, involving employees in the technology integration process enhances buy-in and creates a shared vision for the future.

In preparing for emerging technologies, strategic foresight becomes a crucial skill. Leaders must develop the ability to anticipate potential disruptions and opportunities, responding with agility and resilience. This involves scanning the horizon for new trends, understanding the implications of technological shifts, and crafting strategic responses that align with long-term business objectives.

The logic of emerging technologies also underscores the importance of adaptability. Leaders must remain open to changing paths, adjusting strategies as new information becomes available. Cultivating a mindset that embraces change and encourages experimentation can position organizations to not only withstand disruptive forces but also leverage them as a source of competitive advantage.

As technology continues to evolve at a rapid pace, so does the notion of leadership. The upcoming era will likely demand a new breed of leaders who can navigate the intricate dance between human empathy and technological efficiency. Those who succeed will be the ones who understand the symbiotic relationship between people and technology, ensuring that advancements in the latter serve to enhance and elevate the former.

The future of digital leadership is as much about preparing for technological advancements as it is about fostering the human elements that will always be at the heart of influence and authority. Leaders must strive to cultivate an environment where curiosity thrives, innovation is continuous, and technology acts as an enabler of human potential. In the end, leadership in the digital age will be defined by those who can balance the power of innovation with the essence of humanity.

## Envisioning New Leadership Paradigms

The landscape of leadership, like the sands of time, is eternally shifting, reshaped by the winds of technological advancement. As we stand on the precipice of unprecedented change, new leadership paradigms are emerging, demanding that we not only adapt but also innovate. The leaders of tomorrow are tasked with envisioning a future where leadership isn't merely reactive but dynamic and forward-thinking. This vision involves embracing fluidity, fostering inclusivity, and leveraging technology to create value and meaning in ways we once thought unimaginable.

In this ever-evolving digital era, the lines between the leader and the led are blurring. Hierarchies, once the foundation of organizational structure, are giving way to more networked and agile models. This shift calls for leaders who are less gatekeepers and more facilitators. The traditional command-and-control style, omnipresent in the boardrooms of the past, is being replaced by a model that values collaboration and co-creation with teams. It's less about issuing directives and more about cultivating environments where creativity and innovation thrive.

Envisioning these new paradigms requires an understanding that leadership in the digital age is about curating collective intelligence. With the wealth of information available at their fingertips, leaders must act as navigators, guiding their organizations through complex, data-laden environments. They need to be adept at discerning and synthesizing insights, extracting wisdom from data noise, and translating that into strategic actions that propel their organizations forward. In this way, a leader becomes a synthesizer of ideas, a collaborator who draws on diverse perspectives to craft strategies that are both informed and innovative.

This paradigm shift also involves redefining the skills and attributes necessary for effective leadership. Emotional intelligence, once viewed as ancillary, now sits at the core of leadership excellence. The ability to empathize, to understand and relate to others, is paramount. Digital leaders need to demonstrate agility in thinking and approach, effortlessly pivoting in response to rapidly changing circumstances. They must be open to learning and unlearning, willing to challenge their own biases and assumptions in the pursuit of growth.

A critical component of this new paradigm is inclusivity. The eight billion voices in our interconnected world each hold unique perspectives, experiences, and insights. Effective digital leadership capitalizes on this diversity by creating spaces where these voices can be heard and valued. Empowering individuals from varied backgrounds to contribute to the organization's goals not only enriches decision-making but also drives innovation and fosters a more engaged and harmonious workplace.

Furthermore, leaders must navigate the ethical challenges posed by digital transformation. With great power comes great responsibility—this adage holds truer now than ever. As leaders experiment with AI, big data, and other cutting-edge technologies, they must weigh the ethical implications of their decisions. How we use technology reflects our values and can significantly impact society. A leader's duty is to ensure that technology serves humanity, instead of allowing humanity to become subservient to technology.

Collaboration across sectors is becoming apparent in these new paradigms. Leaders need to recognize that the challenges of the future—ranging from climate change to cybersecurity threats—cannot be solved in isolation. By building networks of collaboration across industries, leaders can not only harness the collective power of innovation but also align diverse interests to confront global challenges effectively. This interconnected mindset is essential for fostering resilience and ensuring sustainable growth in a volatile world.

To cultivate these new paradigms, formal education and traditional leadership development programs are taking a backseat to continuous learning and experiential knowledge-gathering. Leaders are realizing that to remain relevant, they must be lifelong learners, constantly engaging with emerging trends and technologies. From online courses to peer networks, the pathways to learning have broadened, offering leaders a plethora of ways to stay ahead of the curve.

As we look toward the horizon, envisioning new leadership paradigms also involves embracing disruption. Innovation often arises out of chaos, and today's digital leaders must be willing to ride the waves of disruption, using them as opportunities to reinvent and redefine organizational success. In this context, resilience becomes a keystone. Leaders who possess the tenacity to weather digital storms and the foresight to pivot quickly will ensure their organizations not only survive but thrive in the face of adversity.

In summary, the future of digital leadership is characterized by a blend of vision, adaptability, inclusivity, and ethical responsibility. It's about fostering environments that are conducive to innovation, where diverse voices can contribute to collective success. As we envision these new paradigms, we must remain anchored to the principles that ensure technology enhances human potential while advancing the goals of our organizations. In doing so, we set the stage for a future where leadership is not just about influencing and guiding, but about inspiring and transforming.

# Chapter 24:
## Case Studies in Digital Leadership

A s we delve into the world of digital leadership, the stories of those who've navigated this uncharted territory provide invaluable lessons. From the visionary strategies of tech giants to the innovative maneuvers of entrepreneurial startups, digital trailblazers showcase how to wield influence in today's interconnected landscapes. These case studies reveal the synthesis of bold ideas and strategic acumen, offering both success stories and cautionary tales that underscore the highs and lows of digital transformation. For instance, the rise of social media influencers reshaping entire industries illustrates the power of personal brand authenticity, while the collapse of certain tech startups serves as a lesson in ethical oversight and sustainable growth. Together, these narratives highlight the complexities of leadership amidst digital disruption, illustrating the delicate balance between innovation and resilience. They're not just tales of triumph or failure; they are blueprints for navigating the volatile waters of tech-driven change, encouraging today's leaders to adapt, learn, and lead with a forward-thinking mindset.

## Learning from Digital Trailblazers

Digital trailblazers are the modern-day pioneers charting new courses in the technology-driven landscape. Their journeys often serve as roadmaps for navigating the challenges and opportunities that arise in a hyperconnected world. These individuals embody the attributes of strategic risk-taking, relentless innovation, and adaptability—qualities that have historically propelled societies forward during pivotal epochs. To truly grasp the essence of digital leadership, one must examine the paths forged by these visionary leaders who consistently push the boundaries and redefine the standards of success.

Consider, for example, the early adapters of social media platforms who understood the potential of digital networks to transform communication and connectivity. Mark Zuckerberg's establishment of Facebook, for instance, was more than just the creation of a platform for social interaction. It was a decisive move that revolutionized the way people connect, communicate, and consume information. By recognizing the shifting tides of digital interaction, Zuckerberg catalyzed a new era where social platforms are not only sources of entertainment but also pivotal arenas for global discourse and information dissemination.

Similarly, look at Elon Musk, whose ventures embody the quintessential traits of a digital trailblazer. Through Tesla and SpaceX, Musk has ventured into territories that many deemed improbable. His vision for sustainable energy and space exploration challenges established industries and promotes innovation as a driver of change. By prioritizing bold objectives over traditional limitations, Musk exemplifies how leaders in the digital age can leverage technology to accomplish what was once thought impossible.

Ultimately, what sets these trailblazers apart is their ability to envision potential where others see obstacles. They understand that in the digital age, stagnation is synonymous with obsolescence. Their experiences teach us that embracing change is not merely an option but a necessity. Leaders must be receptive to the ever-evolving landscape, ready to pivot and embrace new trends and technologies as they emerge. This agility enables them to constructively harness the power of digital platforms and technological advancements.

Beyond individual leaders, entire organizations have also demonstrated pioneering prowess. Netflix's metamorphosis from a DVD rental service to a global streaming behemoth illustrates the power of digital transformation. By anticipating the rise of digital media consumption, Netflix redefined entertainment and disrupted traditional broadcasting models. This evolution underscores the importance of foresight and agility in maintaining relevance and attaining significant market share in the digital economy.

In a similar vein, Amazon's relentless expansion from an online bookstore to a multifaceted global enterprise exemplifies strategic growth in the digital domain. Jeff Bezos' insight into the e-commerce potential, coupled with an enduring commitment to customer-centric innovation, laid the groundwork for Amazon's monumental ascent. The company's unwavering focus on technology and seamless consumer experience serves as a paradigm for how digital leaders can forge sustainable competitive advantage.

Despite the spotlight on digital successes, it's vital to also derive lessons from the missteps and failures of certain digital initiatives. The collapse of companies like Theranos offers cautionary tales of hubris and deception, reminding leaders of the importance of transparency and ethical integrity. In an era where trust is built and broken at the speed of a tweet, maintaining an authentic and ethical digital presence is paramount for long-term success.

As digital leaders continue to emerge, their journeys offer invaluable insights into the artistry of digital leadership. Aspiring leaders should observe how trailblazers manage to unify strategic vision with technological acumen and, crucially, how they master the delicate balance between innovation and ethical responsibility. By learning from their successes and acknowledging their failures, we can gain a comprehensive understanding of what it takes to lead in our increasingly digital world.

The ability to adapt, innovate, and consistently lead with integrity will become even more crucial as new technologies continue to reshape the landscape. Whether through the development of groundbreaking products or the cultivation of inclusive online communities, digital trailblazers offer blueprints for how to thrive amidst technological disruption. Observing and learning from these pioneers equips new generations of leaders with the tools they need to write their own success stories in the digital age.

The stories of these digital pioneers inspire us to ask ourselves pivotal questions. What changes can you champion within your own organization to align with the shifting digital landscape? How can you leverage emerging technologies to solve existing challenges or create new opportunities? Ultimately, while the trailblazers provide guidance, each leader must chart their own path—navigating uncertainties and seizing the possibilities that lie beyond the horizon.

## Success Stories and Cautionary Tales

In the digital age, leadership doesn't merely reflect traditional paradigms but evolves continuously, strategically merging foresight with flexibility. This evolution is evident in the numerous success stories that have carved pathways for today's digital leaders. Leaders who adapt Machiavellian principles to the digital landscape have consistently demonstrated resilience, innovation, and influence, underlining essential qualities that shape successful digital leadership.

Consider the story of a tech entrepreneur who took the gaming world by storm. With a keen understanding of digital power dynamics, they transformed a passion project into a multi-million-dollar company, largely by crafting a magnetic online persona and leveraging the reach of social media platforms. Their success lay not just in a robust digital strategy but in their ability to read emerging trends and respond adeptly. By analyzing user data and feedback, they fine-tuned the gaming experience, illustrating the powerful blend of data-driven decision-making with emotional intelligence.

Contrast this with a narrative marked by caution. An ambitious CEO, determined to disrupt the e-commerce sector, invested heavily in cutting-edge technology without adequately prioritizing ethical concerns or transparency with consumers. As privacy issues surfaced, consumer trust plummeted, triggering a backlash that led to significant reputational damage. This cautionary tale underscores the critical importance of balancing innovation with ethical responsibility, a lesson for any leader in the digital sphere.

A notable success in leadership is seen in the story of a global fashion brand that embraced digital connectivity to revitalize its market presence. The brand successfully navigated cultural nuances and expanded its influence across continents by engaging with diverse digital communities. The secret to their success was not just in strategic marketing but in respecting and adapting to local digital cultures, exemplifying how digital leadership can cross cultural boundaries effectively.

On the flip side, a prominent software company faced challenges when attempting to expand its operations globally without thoroughly understanding the digital cultures it was entering. The company's initial oversight resulted in culturally insensitive campaigns that alienated potential customers. This scenario serves as a warning against underestimating the significance of cultural intelligence in digital leadership. Successful leaders must recognize that understanding and integrating local cultures is key to leading across digital borders.

In the realm of crisis management, tech leaders have found their mettle tested, with each challenge providing valuable lessons. One particularly successful case involved a social media platform that adeptly handled a major data breach by swiftly performing damage control while maintaining transparency with its user base. They quickly introduced enhanced security measures, which not only mitigated the crisis but also restored user confidence and loyalty. This success story highlights the crucial role of prompt responsiveness and clear communication in maintaining authority during digital crises.

By contrast, a leading cybersecurity firm's failure to effectively manage a similar breach resulted in devastating consequences. The firm's delayed response and lack of transparent communication fueled public mistrust and undermined its core mission of safeguarding digital assets. This cautionary tale emphasizes that the inability to act quickly and communicate effectively in a crisis can severely damage a leader's reputation and authority in the digital landscape.

Innovation and adaptability drive successful digital leadership, yet cautionary examples remind us that these traits must be wielded wisely. The dynamic tech company that launched an innovative AI-driven product without fully assessing its potential societal impact soon found itself entangled in ethical controversy. Users were concerned about privacy and data misuse, leading to massive public outcry. This cautionary incident underscores the necessity of ethical foresight in innovation, ensuring technology serves humanity, not the other way around.

Success stories in digital leadership also involve fostering and maintaining engaged virtual teams. A successful example is a multinational enterprise that prioritized collaboration and inclusivity by utilizing digital tools to create a cohesive and motivated virtual team. By fostering a culture of openness and innovation, the company's leaders ensured high levels of engagement and productivity, demonstrating how effective leadership can cultivate thriving digital work environments.

Conversely, the tale of an organization that failed to support its virtual workforce highlights potential pitfalls. Despite having access to advanced digital communication tools, the lack of team engagement and unclear expectations led to discontent and decreased productivity. This situation serves as a cautionary tale against neglecting the human aspect of digital teamwork, reminding leaders that digital tools are only as effective as the relationships and trust that underpin them.

Both the triumphs and failures in digital leadership serve as critical learning tools. Each success story inspires new methodologies for embracing digital innovation, while cautionary tales warn against the common pitfalls that can derail even the most technologically advanced initiatives. The key for modern leaders lies in synthesizing these insights to craft a balanced, adaptable leadership approach that honors the guiding principles of the past while embracing the possibilities of the future.

In their pursuit of mastery, digital leaders must remain vigilant, open to learning from both successful innovations and the challenges faced by others. This continuous learning attitude not only fosters adaptive strategies but also ensures that leaders can effectively navigate the complexities and rapid changes inherent in the digital world. As we study more trailblazers who brilliantly balance the art and science of digital leadership, we understand that the most profound achievements often arise from the seamless integration of strategic vision and ethical commitment.

# Chapter 25:
# Mastering the Art of
# Digital Leadership

In the realm of digital leadership, mastery isn't a destination but a continuous journey, demanding relentless adaptability and insight. The essence of digital leadership lies in synthesizing vast spectra of insights, pulling from diverse digital experiences to forge paths that others have yet to tread. It's about harnessing the ceaseless wave of innovation and turning potential disruption into an opportunity to chart a visionary course. With an eye towards the future, leaders must build a legacy not just on technological prowess but on enduring influence, compelling narratives, and robust networks. By aligning technology with human values, they create ecosystems where digital success and authenticity coexist. To truly master this craft, one must balance the creative and the strategic, ensuring that as each digital footprint is made, it resonates with purpose and forward-thinking vision, leaving a mark that is both influential and inspired in our hyperconnected world.

## Synthesizing Insights

In the digital age, leadership demands more than just a skillful command of modern tools and networks—it requires a synthesis of insights that blend traditional wisdom with cutting-edge innovations. As the threads of technology weave into the very fabric of leadership, it's critical for leaders to step back and integrate the knowledge they've gathered. This synthesis is not just an intellectual exercise but an essential process to master the art of digital leadership.

At the heart of synthesizing insights lies the ability to draw from vast realms of information while maintaining a clear vision. Digital leaders are bombarded with data, metrics, and analytics. The challenge is to transform this avalanche of information into coherent strategies that drive meaningful outcomes. Just as an artist blends colors to create a masterpiece, leaders must amalgamate these insights into actionable pathways that are both innovative and grounded in reality.

Effective synthesis hinges on recognizing patterns that others might overlook. It's about connecting the seemingly disparate dots to reveal a bigger picture that informs strategic decisions. Leaders must cultivate a mindset of curiosity, consistently questioning and exploring beyond the obvious. This not only aids in better understanding complex digital dynamics but also uncovers unique opportunities that position organizations ahead in the competitive landscape.

Moreover, the skill of synthesizing insights is deeply aligned with agility and adaptability. In a rapidly changing digital environment, the ability to pivot based on fresh insights can distinguish thriving leaders from those who falter. Quick, nimble responses to emerging trends create resilience. Yet, this requires having a strategy in place that's flexible, allowing room for iteration and growth without losing sight of the core objectives.

Leadership in the digital world also revolves around shared knowledge and collaborative innovation. The insights gathered are more powerful when they evolve through open dialogue and shared experiences. By creating platforms where teams can contribute and critique, a collective intelligence emerges—one that is richer and more nuanced than individual understanding. Encouraging such collaborative frameworks fosters a culture of inclusivity and opens the pathways to diverse perspectives.

Nevertheless, synthesis isn't merely an act of merging existing knowledge. It involves foreseeing the implications of novel ideas and disruptive technologies. Leaders must anticipate the ripple effects of their decisions within the broader socio-technical ecosystem. This foresight not only mitigates risks associated with rapid technological advancement but also ensures that the benefits of innovation are aligned with humanitarian goals and ethical standards.

A meaningful synthesis of insights also requires embracing contradictions. In the digital age, complexities abound, and leaders need to be comfortable with ambiguity. Effective leadership involves balancing conflicting interests—innovating while preserving values, leveraging technology while ensuring human interaction remains central. This paradoxical thinking, reminiscent of Machiavellian strategies adapted to modern times, becomes vital in navigating these challenges.

Ultimately, synthesizing insights is a process that equates knowledge with wisdom. It requires reflection, discernment, and action. Leaders must remain vigilant, continuously learning and unlearning to adapt their practice to the changing tides. This dynamic interplay of gathering, integrating, and applying insights becomes a cornerstone of transformative leadership.

In looking towards the future, those who succeed will be those who can harness this synthesis to inspire, guide, and enact positive change. Masterful leaders will not only build upon the legacies of the past but also forge new paradigms of leadership that resonate with the demands of a hyperconnected and tech-driven world.

What emerges is a landscape where digital leaders synthesize not just to react, but to innovate actively, and chart new paths. This proactive approach breeds leaders who are not merely spectators of change but architects of a digitally-enhanced future. As we move forward, the challenge is clear but so is the opportunity for those prepared to master the art of synthesizing insights.

## Building Your Legacy

In the grand tapestry of digital leadership, building your legacy stands as both the capstone and cornerstone of one's journey. It's not just about building empires, but rather about creating lasting impacts that transcend the immediate and echo into the future. As Machiavelli suggested, the end goal of power isn't mere control—it's enduring influence. In today's hyperconnected digital sphere, where information travels at the speed of a click, the essence of a leader's legacy is now more visible and scrutinized than ever before.

To build a legacy, modern digital leaders must first understand the unique tools and platforms available to them. They must learn to wield these with precision. The digital world provides an unprecedented opportunity to document one's vision, values, and victories. Leaders can preserve their philosophies through blogs, podcasts, and even social media, ensuring their insights persist long after their tenure.

However, the true measure of a legacy isn't in the quantity of content shared, but in the quality of the connections and communities built. Digital leaders must nurture environments where ideas can flourish and where followers are inspired to engage and innovate. This environment promotes an ethos of shared success—after all, a legacy is not something one builds alone. It's a collaboration with those you lead and influence.

Great leaders have always known the importance of mentorship, and in the digital age, this tradition continues albeit in a new form. Digital platforms allow leaders to mentor from afar, offering guidance that is not bound by geographical limitations. By integrating mentorship into their legacy-building strategy, leaders ensure that their values and knowledge are continuously passed down. They plant seeds of growth and innovation across the globe, allowing their influence to extend far beyond their immediate sphere.

The challenge for digital leaders lies in harmonizing authenticity with adaptability. A legacy is not about rigid adherence to one's initial vision; it's about evolving while holding fast to core principles. Leaders must navigate the delicate balance between staying true to their values and adapting those values to new contexts and challenges. By doing so, they don't just respond to change; they shape it.

Another critical component of building a legacy is ethical leadership. In the digital era, where information can be manipulated and privacy concerns abound, leaders must prioritize transparency and integrity. Ethical decisions lay the groundwork for a legacy built on trust and respect. As followers increasingly demand accountability, leaders who proactively address ethical issues will find their legacies strengthened, while those who neglect such issues may see theirs tarnished.

The legacy of a digital leader also involves equipping future leaders with the skills they need. This means fostering a culture of continuous learning and encouraging curiosity. By promoting lifelong learning, leaders ensure that their legacy of innovation and adaptability is carried forward. This not only helps in nurturing future leaders but also secures the leader's contributions to their field, echoing long after they have stepped away.

A digital leader's legacy isn't just about forging a path but also about envisioning pathways for others. By enabling rather than dictating, they ensure their influence empowers others to lead. This establishes a chain of transformative leadership that can redefine industries and communities alike.

In these rapidly evolving times, flexibility is crucial. A leader's legacy will be defined as much by their adaptability to new technologies as by their foundational principles. Thus, a legacy is both a reflection of a leader's past achievements and an indication of how they have poised the next generation for future success.

Finally, a digital legacy doesn't just live in the memory of those it has touched directly. It lives in the data. The actions, reactions, and impacts can be analyzed, critiqued, and incorporated into future frameworks. Tech-driven tools like analytics and insight reporting provide a means for leaders to continuously refine their strategies and ensure their legacy is not just remembered but actively utilized.

In sum, building one's legacy as a digital leader is about crafting a narrative that's both influential and inspirational. It's about creating a lasting impact that aligns with the leader's ethos while preparing others to carry the baton forward. From embracing innovation to fostering ethical standards, leaders must be mindful architects of their digital legacies. In doing so, they lay the foundation for a world that continues to benefit from their vision and leadership long after they've concluded their direct journey.

# Conclusion

In weaving the timeless principles of Machiavellian philosophy into the fabric of our digital age, we find a roadmap for leadership that is as relevant today as it was in Renaissance Italy. The journey through this book has, we hope, illuminated the path to becoming an effective digital leader, one who commands influence and respect in an increasingly interconnected world.

As leaders, the challenge before us is not merely to adapt but to embrace the ongoing transformation that technology fosters. The lessons of digital leadership demand a nimbleness of mind, a willingness to engage with the relentless pace of change, and a keen understanding of the power dynamics that shape our virtual landscapes. These skills are not just desirable; they are essential for anyone aiming to leave a lasting impact in the digital realm.

Reflect on the idea of influence. In the digital age, influence is no longer restricted by geography or limited by traditional hierarchies. It's a force that can be cultivated through strategic engagement across various platforms. Crafting an authentic online persona and leveraging social media are not just modern methods of communication—they are vital strategies in asserting authority and building networks of support and collaboration.

Moreover, the digital leader must become an adept persuader, capable of crafting messages that resonate in a world inundated with information. This is a skill honed not only by understanding your audience and their needs but by building genuine trust. In a virtual world, trust becomes a cornerstone upon which relationships—and reputations—are built.

Decision-making in a time of information overload presents another unique challenge. The plethora of data at our fingertips can both empower and overwhelm. Thus, the digital leader must cultivate the ability to sift through the noise, making informed decisions quickly and accurately, while balancing speed with caution.

Ethical challenges will continue to evolve, intensifying as technology advances. Modern leaders are called upon to navigate these waters with a moral compass that balances transparency with innovation. It's not a simple task but an essential part of building ethical leadership practices that align with both organizational objectives and societal expectations.

Navigating crises, fostering innovation, and managing virtual teams are further aspects every digital leader will confront. It's in these scenarios where resilience, creativity, and engagement become your most powerful allies. Knowing when to stand firm and when to adapt is a test that calls on both instinct and strategic foresight.

Technology equips us with tools unimaginable in the past, yet their effective use depends on our ability to integrate them into our leadership practices purposefully. Leaders must be relentless learners, ever-curious about new technologies and ever-ready to adapt their strategies to harness these tools effectively.

As the digital landscape evolves, so must our understanding of cultural, social, and global dynamics. Leadership today is not constrained by borders; it requires a mindful approach to diversity, inclusiveness, and cultural sensitivity.

Moreover, our exploration of AI and automation reminds us of the delicate balance we must maintain between leveraging technological advances and preserving our human touch. These tools should enhance our leadership, not overshadow it. The goal is to ensure that technology serves humanity, enriching rather than diminishing our connections.

Thinking forward, the future of digital leadership is bright but demands readiness for emerging technologies and a reimagining of leadership paradigms. How we embrace these shifts will determine our effectiveness and legacy in this digital era.

Although this book draws to a close, the journey of mastering digital leadership is continuous. Each leader must synthesize these insights uniquely, crafting a legacy that reflects both personal mission and the larger human story. To lead effectively in the digital realm is to blend art with strategy, vision with execution, and ambition with ethics.

In conclusion, every leader stands at the threshold of a new era where opportunities to excel abound. The principles laid out in this book—rooted in historical wisdom yet steeped in modern relevance—are your companions as you embark on your own journey of digital leadership. Strive to be not just a leader, but a trailblazer who shapes the future and inspires others to follow.

# Appendix A:
# Appendix (if needed)

In the evolving landscape of digital leadership, the journey doesn't end with the strategies outlined in this book. Instead, it continues with the practical application of these principles in diverse situations that modern leaders encounter. This appendix serves as a supplementary guide, offering additional insights that complement the core content to equip you with further resources for mastering influence and navigating power dynamics in the digital realm.

Much like Machiavelli's observations on the intricate nature of human behavior, our contemporary world requires a nuanced understanding of both technology and humanity. The insights here aim to bridge gaps that you might encounter as you apply theoretical concepts to real-world challenges.

**Additional Readings:** Delve deeper into the transformative power of digital tools with a curated list of additional readings that explore diverse aspects of leadership in a hyperconnected age.

**Practical Exercises:** Engage with exercises designed to refine your digital leadership skills. These exercises encourage self-reflection, problem-solving, and strategic thinking.

**Resources for Continued Learning:** Stay informed about the latest trends and innovations in digital leadership. This section lists useful platforms, podcasts, and newsletters that will keep you up-to-date.

**Glossary of Terms:** Familiarize yourself with critical terminology that has been used throughout the book. Understanding these terms will enhance your comprehension of digital leadership concepts.

Embrace the ever-changing digital environment with confidence. Let this appendix guide you in expanding your perspective, reinforcing your knowledge, and applying Machiavellian strategies in an ethical and modern context. Remember, the key to leadership in today's world lies not just in knowledge but in the continuous pursuit of growth and adaptability.

www.ingramcontent.com/pod-product-compliance
Lightning Source LLC
Chambersburg PA
CBHW051236050326
40689CB00007B/938